Divine
Horse-icity

Washerpop Davidson

ISBN:1546751122
ISBN-13:9781546751120

DEDICATION

I have dedicated this book to my ghost writer, and human friend; Hannah Davidson. I have autonomy but apparently, I am not to be trusted with the laptop. And to my friend and brother in arms, Henry Bear; I have an odd way of showing my appreciation for you, to you, but your bum is so fine I just have to bite it.

CONTENTS

ACKNOWLEDGMENTS

I would like to thank the lovely ones who pass by my field and feed Henry and I carrots. I already thanked Hannah for interpreting and writing this book for me, I will not thank her twice, she can get big headed.

FORWARD BY HANNAH DAVIDSON

"That's the real trouble with the world; too many people grew up." ~
Walt Disney

On first getting to know Washerpop, I did not know it would lead to me ghost writing this book for him, I would like to say a few words first because for the rest of this book you will get a raw and in no way understated horse's eye view of things. This horse has been generous enough to gift me with his passionate view of things, he has been undying in his devotion to my understanding, and unrelenting in his enthusiasm for teaching me.

It has felt punishing at times, like when he would get half way around a ride and didn't want to carry on but did not want to go home either! Or the endless times he would come charging up to me in the field, apparently ecstatic to see me and then refuse to walk in to the stable yard with me. I would give up, take the halter off and walk away, only then feel the delightfulness of his warm breath on the back of my neck as he would follow me to the gate.

But truly he has shown me amongst everything else that you will read about here, that integrity such as his is something that most of us humans remember little of. We often have it obliterated from our minds as children, as we learn that growing up means compromise; that dreams are silly, but that hard work and conformity are what makes you a successful proper grown up.

We learn that it is acceptable to ride roughshod over others feelings, because we have had our own feelings ignored or belittled so often that this appears now to be the normal state of affairs, an institutionalization of sorts.

We are taught to please others before we please ourselves and then wonder why we are bent over backwards never being able to do enough to keep the people around us happy, while rarely finding any fulfilment for ourselves. We lose our playfulness and can surrender our ability to have integrity as we start to agree with the adults that the world is the way it is, that in essence we have to accept the stuff we don't like and just get on with it.

This attitude, these low standards we acquire for ourselves, in how we allow others, and life in general to treat us, end up being the measures that in turn, we put onto those around us, the ones that we love. We start to see that if we don't get a result that we want, the answer is to push harder for it. Not often do we learn that if things are not going in the desired direction, that maybe we are going the wrong way about it. Maybe we could change our viewpoint and our way of going about things instead of continuously wearing ourselves out by grinding up against the things we do not wish to be present in our reality.

Also, we rarely question if what we want is what would genuinely make us happy or if it is other people's ideas of what success means, that is driving us.

Washerpop dared to dream; he dared to dream that a human could give him something different, something other than the mediocrity of surrendering his feelings, his life; having his wants and needs being ridden roughshod over in the name of being 'given a job', being 'taught manners' being made 'safe to handle' or even in the name of my very altruistic desire to make him into a happy and well-adjusted horse – still – yet still – he showed me that what I considered would make him happy, was not the point! He, like all of our beasts, already knew, perfectly well how to be happy! He, like all of us, is, in fact, is the only one who can know what does and doesn't float his particular boat!

As human beings, when we are children, the adults in our lives mostly show us that conformity is of value to us. Then as we grow up, others around us, and television, and media imprint the idea that everything - from what clothes we wear to sexual preference should fit into what society deems to be normal. We stifle our creativity and individuality and accept less for ourselves.

Too easily we become less of our individual selves, and we think it is acceptable to push everything else around us into a conventional shaped mould. The human race as a whole very rarely considers that any animals may have individual wants and needs, if you look at modern farming today; it tells us everything about how little we value any other beings right to have something in life that has not been chosen for them by another.

But still, this horse; my Washerpop did not want to be "left to it" out in the field either.

He would always come to me delighted to play the human games but would let me know straight away if something was off in my approach, and off for him, could mean anything as simple as my mind being elsewhere, or the opposite; me focusing on him too intensely.

Washerpop has a good sense of his importance, he will not engage his mind and body for someone who is not wholly present and correct in their self, and at the opposite end of the scale; my beady eye could be too intent - no one likes to be scrutinized!

This horse gave me a glimmer of hope. I was quietly horrified and in awe at the same time; of his unashamed knowing of his rightness and his different and very inventive ways of showing me how he wanted to choose his life and not just allow it to be swept away on a human whim.

Once I had got past my feeling that he was completely insane and untrainable, I started to see the things I had forgotten but known as a child.

I saw and felt Washers keen sense of himself, his utter certainty that he knew what was right for him and that he could perceive he was being fair in standing up for that. He was not doing anything at all wrong in following his personal moral code; his intrinsic bliss, exploring his likes and dislikes as we went along. He was so sure, even in what would seem an unclimbable mountain for a horse, he was so sure he could make me truly see him that he made me want to try out his theology for myself.

This knowing one's self, this standing up for one's happiness even if every other may think you wrong or crazy.

I began to think that maybe this horse is some sort of genius.

I remembered how free I felt as a child; I didn't care who saw me land on my head for the tenth time while I practiced my backflips. Washer does not care about the confused/disturbed look on my face when he is taste testing slugs AGAIN! I recalled how Dad would shout for us to come indoors as darkness came, us children being desperate for the day to last a little longer, for the sun not to go down.

If we are now considering our animals in a greater light, do we wish to acknowledge and see more and more of their very real intelligence? the shining light that they bring to us? Would we like to be aware of their needs and wants on a subtler level, a deeper level? More akin to that which we like and need for ourselves to feel fulfilled in life once our basic needs of food, shelter and warmth are satisfied? If the answer is Yes, then we can begin to co-create with our creatures in a new way, a way that allows for immense evolution for humankind, but also for our animals, and brings with it a vast amount of satisfaction for all.

In fact, I will go as far as to say; considering our animals on a deeper level is not actually what needs to come first. Washer showed me that we do not have enough consideration for ourselves; we do not have high enough expectations from life, so certainly are not prepared to think our animals may have high expectancy, or have a right to more.

I am saying; "our" animals, not in a proprietary way, but because anything not domesticated at some level can choose whether to interact with humans or not, whereas animals we elect to "keep" mostly do not have that choice. As Antione de Saint-Exupery says in his fabulous book; The Little Prince: "Nous sommes responsables pour ceux qui nous avons apprivous." It means: you become responsible forever for what you have tamed.

They are 'ours' if they are in our lives and our hearts and us in theirs.

All of our animals are like us; individuals, who have personal tastes, likes, dislikes, wants and needs aside from, or as well as, their breed or species characteristics that may also define them. They too, like us can suffer and feel burdened if forced like a square peg in a round hole.

Washerpop indeed would feel very indignant at any disapproval of him on my part. He will never allow me to quash his feeling without letting me know about it and for that, I can never thank him enough. Washer has at every turn given me the opportunity to think about what I am doing, what I want and for me to consider his point of view. I have by no means understood or agreed with his point of view on many occasions, but the important thing was, to acknowledge that he has one (a point of view that is) and that he has a right to have one that is differing to mine!

Something important that we humans often do not recognize or acknowledge is that no two beings; human, horse or otherwise can have the same opinion about everything. We have all come to this particular point in time through our various experiences of life. We are all looking into the house from different windows and seeing a different part of the room, so to speak. And we all come with our own very varied personalities, so two who are experiencing the same thing can have opposing views on it.

I have had discussions with my younger sister about events that happened with us both as children and we look back on these and see them very differently sometimes. Some things that have meant the most to me are sometimes not even remembered by my sister and vice versa.

Some experiences, one of us recalls as a happy time and the other does not.

If we cannot acknowledge another's differing point of view, any relationship only consists of telling, or bribing, or cajoling the other into thinking our ideas and opinions are good ones. Once we can start to allow opinions that differ to ours, then we can learn, and experience what happens when we give our animals a genuine choice in their interactions with us.

You will be surprised and delighted at how, if another being is allowed the choice as to whether to interact and co-create with you and they do say yes to that, how wonderfully they will reward you with their whole being.

What Washer has shown me IS there for everyone, we just need to get out of our own way to allow this energy to flow, for this relationship to develop. When our animals can feel free to express themselves without judgement or punishment, then we have proper engagement. (And yes, they do sense our judgement upon them) If we can stop trying to drive ourselves down a narrow set path and instead be open to allowing our horses to offer us things, you may find as I have, that you are utterly overthrown with humility, love and appreciation for the gifts your horse will give you on his terms. There is a harmonious balance where a mutual give and take occurs that has nothing at all to do with "submission" or "behaving" or the horse "respecting" us.

If your horse sees you are trustworthy of sharing his whole self with you, then he will do that.

And then our animals can see us as we want them to see us; as good friends, good fun, trustworthy and worth spending time with. Most people think that if you give a horse the choice of only doing what he wants, then he will choose to do nothing but eat the grass with his buddies. Washer has shown me the opposite to be true. That given the choice of interacting with humans or being left to "horse" in the field, if the interaction and riding allow him the choice of participation and come with no conditions, then he is delighted to spend time with me, to be ridden, and to show his best self to me.

The natural, wholesome relationships we had with our animals as children are something a lot of us look back to, wistful of that pure beauty we managed to effortlessly attain before growing up and becoming "responsible adults" and learning to take life seriously.

But, you know what has changed since then? Only that we grew up and took on the "I know best for you!" role, and that attitude takes away any chance at proper friendship.

Most of us have probably had a friend (or relative) at some point who did not like our choice of new partner. And what happened? Head over heels, falling in love, your attention on nothing but following what feels good regardless of potential outcomes, and there is your friend, maybe not even saying it out loud, but boring into you with that feeling of:

"I know best for you, and it's not him! (or her)".

Let me guess, you didn't like that friend so much hey? And you wanted to say to them;

"my life, my choice! Butt out of my business!"

I bet you if things did go wrong; that friend was the last person you would want to confide in, only to get a "I told you so" from them.

To achieve the relationship I wanted with Washer, I did have to allow him the choice. I did have to let him out in that field and say; "Hey Wash if you don't want to do human stuff, ever again, it is fine with me; I will love you and do my best to look after you anyway".

And believe me, he did test that I meant that to the highest! And it did bring into question my motives and desires.

Some people also make a distinction with their horses that you can't just be friends and achieve stuff; 'being versus doing'. or that we need to make a choice between being friends and being "in charge" or "respected."

This thinking, that if you only want to cuddle your equine and feed them carrots, and maybe teach the odd trick or two then that is fine to put friendship first. But if you want a competition horse, you want one brave and safe enough to jump big fences or robust and supple enough to perform all of the fancy dressage moves, then you need to set down boundaries and ground rules.

You have to push them as you push yourselves; through physical and mental barriers, and this is where we take away consent. Where there is hard work to be done, and the horse has to participate even if he has a reason not to want to, here is a problem. If he is not physically or mentally able on any one particular day, but we grind ahead anyway, then this is taking our human concept that 'only hard work achieves and that shirkers get nowhere', and pushing that concept onto the animal.

I have found it to be a false premise anyway. You will mostly be nowhere else but in a position of assuming the role of motivator, to cajole or even bully because you have decided on a role/regime for your horse, that your horse may not have signed up to. Or the horse may enjoy the work but have a need not to participate on certain days, and this does not fit your regime, so pushing through occurs and consent is taken away.

Taking away of consent by assuming it is there because it was there one time before, is not how the magic, the dance, the entwining of two souls comes about.

I have also found that the use of a stick is not needed, and I am talking about using it for direction and encouragement of forward motion, not punishment. As I have learnt; on the days that Washer felt unable to completely give himself physically or emotionally, I gave him the benefit of the doubt. His little (or sometimes big) protestations listened to instead of punished or pushed through, and he was allowed a day or two or a week off, or we did something different that he did feel enthusiasm for.

I did not allow fear to provoke the thought in me, that he would pull a fast one on me forever more if I did not get on at him; that cynical mindset that says he will become idle and want to do less and less if I do not push for what I want. I found that he would be so overwhelmingly grateful to have had a human listen to him, that he gave me all of his beauty, energy and grace unasked for the next time, no cajoling or whip needed.

Changing how we perceive our animals doesn't mean we can't train, compete or achieve those kinds of things with them. But if we create a balance of emotional wellness within ourselves and our animals, and train with the horse's valid consent every step of the way, our opportunities are limitless.

I could have asked Washerpop to win me rosettes; I could have strapped his mouth shut and pushed him forwards with my legs and the whip, cajoling him and rewarded him greatly for his efforts. I see people do this all of the time and they win stuff. I could have asked him to accept his lot in life as the lesser being that is expected to defer to the human's desires.

And I would have been applauded (as I was for a while) by my peers, for "mastering" such a difficult animal.

I could have said to Washerpop; "this is the life I have chosen for you, you are the horse and I am the human, so I get to decide, and I have decided we are going to achieve in a way that shows the outside world that we have worth because that is the most important thing to us humans. Most of us are nothing without outside praise from others; this is what I have learnt, we must please others! So Washer: you have to buy in. And you shall like it, for I will consider myself kind in my efforts". Ha!

We have not gone together and won any competitions; that is not to say we may not go and do those things in the future if it's something we both think would be fun to explore rather than a need to prove something. Prince Washerpop the 1st does like to show off, and he does have the best fancy trot!

But do you want to know what Washer has given me that is infinitely more precious than some rosettes or other people telling me "well done"? (And believe me, I used to live for a "well done")

He has shown me how to love unconditionally, how to live in the moment, to laugh and to have all the vitality and passion we were born to have.

Not only has he shown me how to "be" with my horses, and all other beasts, but this has translated into my human relationships too. He has shown me how to be my best self, to simply just "be" without needing to get somewhere else, to some point in the future, where after all of my striving and hard work everything would be perfect, and I would be happy.

You may find that many other humans will not understand you if you choose to embark on this less travelled path, but that lack of understanding is made up for by the few who do understand and by the powerful unmistakable softness you will receive from your beasts. So, do not mind or pay attention to the opinions of those that think you may have lost your mind; they are yet to discover the magic themselves, that is all.

I will hand you over to Prince Washerpop now; you are in good hands (hooves!) have fun. I did.

INTRODUCTION

"She swallowed a horse, she died of course" ~ Anon

I, Prince Washerpop the 1st am a horse, and to some that may mean I am uneducated and un-educatable in certain matters beyond learning to have people ride on my back, or to pull a load. You may think our capabilities end at learning basic manners, tricks and other similar things, and you would be right in a small way, I do not need educating in the ways that a human receives schooling; academically. I do not need to add up how many blades of grass I have, and to be able to work out how many I might need to save for later. I do not need to know a lot of complicated words and tactics to take my fellow horse to court because he ate his dinner and then ate mine.

And not for the reasons you think either.

It is not that I am of lesser intelligence, or that a human will come along and be more able than I, and save up my grass for me for winter, and then put me in a paddock away from the horse that steals my food. That human supposedly doing me a service that I should find honourable because I may go hungry or not experience equality in the wild.

It is because I do not hold such false premise as to think that conditions in the world need to be perfect for me to be able to live a harmonious and prosperous life, unlike a lot of you humans do. This striving for perfection is how you end up in a trap of being unhappy with what you have right here and now, and then you try to replace that hollow feeling, that knowing that something is missing, with the things that are available for to you to purchase in your modern world, and there are so many things!

You may think I am going to tell you that instant gratification is the dirge of today's human society, but I am not. It is just that I can see that most of you are all looking for that gratification in the wrong places, one more alcoholic drink, and one more brand new shiny thing. Or you want the beings around you to miraculously decide to behave in a way that will make you happy, or you want a magically large sum of money to land in your lap, so freedom from the pursuit of those pounds will come at last. Then you will be happy!

My dear human reader friends, I have to tell you, you have got it all arse about face. I told Hannah this time and time again, and I still do remind her occasionally now if she is sending out to me these ridiculous thoughts of lack, that tie her in emotional knots; I tell her: "Stay here and now with me, do not bring this never-never land nonsense to my doorstep!"

You can have your instant gratification, just like I get mine with a bum scratch or the second I feel a change in my human; that change in her vibration/attitude that tells me she has found that place to be able to be receptive to listening to me, and then my heart soars. It will become apparent throughout this book; most of what is stopping you from getting the things you want right away, or pretty darn quick, is your desperation to have them right now. And all that lies behind those thoughts of; I'm not good enough, I should have achieved this already, look at that one over there who has already managed to do this thing.

So, you come to a conclusion; I must be a lesser being, less worthy, or my horse must be stupid or mad or faulty, or I was unlucky enough to be born with less talent than some because I have tried hard. And so on, and so on. And on and on your minds go.

It is a topsy-turvy way of going at things, trust me in that. Human concepts taught to you from "teeny weeny" upwards. All of them misplaced and blocking your progression, flow and ability to have peace and enjoyment in the moment. Do you know that a feeling of joy should not be elusive to you? Look at your cats and dogs; they know how to find it at the drop of a hat! Us horses do too if you have not impinged our way of being so harshly that we are In the same miserable darn boat as you are.

I, Washerpop, know all I need to know, to feel vibrant, full of life, full of love and living, to have balance and harmony, without being taught one single thing from a human. This is why I wanted to write my book through Hannah so that people can know what I know and maybe learn to turn their relationships into something unquestionably worth having, something many of you may never have experienced before, something that feeds your soul.

Happiness is a moving thing; defining moment by moment. It is not, as my darling human Hannah previously thought it was; something in the future to aim for, to be worked hard for, it is not brought about by other beings behaving in a way pleasing to you, and it is not brought about by sacrifice.

A horse is born knowing how to 'horse' and it may surprise you to know that you humans are born knowing how to 'human' too! But then you get 'un-humane-ed' as your grownups put you through a system of education that shows you how to be a successful member of society, which has not much at all to do with being who you are meant to be. You were supposed to come and shine, as individuals, not to all be made to think the same thoughts, to know the same things, to do the same things as each other. A scale of your school training instils in you a grading. You need to become better than others to be worthy. The focus is on good and bad, and right or wrong, better or worse, you define your whole lives by these things.

Think about the word humane. It means; 'having or showing compassion or benevolence'. Funny, how you have this word that is supposed to define your species. Where is the room for compassion in a world where you learn that the ones at the top are the only ones to have led a life worth living and that getting to the top of the pile is the whole point of life?

Most of your species are able to see pictures on your television screens of children drowning off boats, fleeing wars started by people who are, or want to be at the top of the pile, and most have nothing more than a fleeting pang about it before it gets pushed it out of your minds, because you think that to jump up and do something humane about it may mean that somebody else may get a step onto your crowded ladder that you have already fought hard to get onto. Humanity is brought down onto its knees over a mistaken place in a queue, having been fooled into indignation and a bun fight over supposedly limited resources.

Think about that. Then you look at a picture of a dog that has been mistreated, and you say to yourself, I am a compassionate person because I would never dream of doing what that person did to that dog.

Measuring yourself again, against others, rather than measuring what you truly have to give, and deep inside want to give, and you may not know it, but those things, you have an unlimited free supply of; love and compassion.

So you are accepting of very low standards to judge yourselves by, and then you are using those as your guidelines in life.

Luckily you have me; Prince Washerpop the 1st.

For I see the world, not through such a small lens, but as a whole, I see and feel the oneness of us all, and I know the greatness inside of myself and inside of each and every one of you. The love you have to give is not finite; you do not have to measure it out or give it out in little bits and pieces here and there and only to those deemed worthy, or only when they please you. It is like the air that you breathe, know it is always there, and know that there is always more than enough to go around.

CHAPTER 1

THE RESCUERS

Penny: Hi. Where'd you come from?

Bernard: We found the bottle with your message, and we've come to rescue you.

Penny: Did you hear that, Teddy? Our bottle worked!

[Looks confused]

Penny: Didn't you bring somebody big with you? Like the police?

Bernard: Uh, no. There's just, uh - the two of us.

Miss Bianca: But if the three of us work together and we have a little faith...

Penny: That's what Rufus said: "Faith makes things turn out right."

The Rescuers – Disney (1977)

I gave my first lesson to Hannah straight off the bat. All of you lovely humans who care so much about your animal friends of all different species will hopefully like this one. Some of you will have defined your life work and may characterise your true self as being rescuers, and or healers, and that is very noble of you.

We know you look around, with your eyes and see much that needs help.

We see you ones striving to give us the best lives, and we gaze on, as you have more doubt and trouble with us on occasion than those who care little for our feelings.

We have much love for you all and would like you to be able to feel and enjoy the fruits of your labour and have the simple, loving, co-operative friendship with us that you at first had in mind.

Hannah discovered that life's expression should not require non-stop effort and grind. It should flow.

I wasn't quite a rescue case, but other people had tried to train me, and I had proved to them to be not very trainable to varying degrees. I was not able to comply with their demands of me because I vigorously know my own identity, I as an individual, while not unhappy to interact with humans, did not come here to serve a purpose for some other being that serves no purpose for me!

I could not understand why I was being asked to do the things the humans wanted. Does it surprise you that we beasts can have the intellect sometimes to want to know why we should be doing what you are asking? Also, I was very young, and my joints would hurt if asked to make tight circles. It was not much fun for me.

Before Hannah and I met, she wanted a challenge. Henry Bear was retiring from being a riding horse after nearly 20 years of wonderful times for them together, riding and being good friends. And so she was looking for a young horse that needed some calmness and kindness and a job of being a riding horse, she thought she would have a lot of love to give to someone like me.

On meeting me, she decided;

1. I was cute

2. I was also pretty darn handsome

3. There is nought wrong with a bit of cheekiness.

She was not what some people call a "tyre kicker" or a "hoof kicker" although if she goes to buy another horse after her experience with me, she may well take brain scanning equipment; "No! – not this one; he has a mind of his own!"

On meeting Hannah, I decided;

1. I liked the zip on her jacket (I like un-zipping humans!)

2. She showed potential

3. Maybe there will be a hot wash and solarium at my new home. I love hot water – Prince Washerpop does not get bathed in cold water!

So I decided to go for it, I could see there was a possibility that I could break this one in, and so she brought me home, she rescued me! To be fair, I had just looked a little anxious and did not have any other equine company where I was – not so big a deal in the grand scheme of things. I had been mooching around a field not doing much of anything for a year. She had learned a little of how I did not appreciate certain ways of training and had been told to steer clear of these.

She had brought me into her life, to make my life better and to gain enjoyment from the new experience and to have a new friend, and these were all good sentiments. Hannah allowed a period for me to settle, but as time moved on she could not work out why having lavished me with love, fabulous food, equine friends, chiropractor and massage treatments, understanding, kindness and calm handlings; I did not seem to want to give her one inch of leeway. Not one of the things she did for me seemed to have earned her so much as a single brownie point! I was not wanting to swap the things she gave, as much as they did delighted me, I did not want to trade those things for handing over my whole self, purely for the humans self-gratification.

I would not turn myself over, despite all the fun I was having because to do that, I would have had to be In total agreement with the human's misconceptions of me, and one of those poorly preconceived ideas of hers; was that she felt sorry for me.

Sorry that I had been misunderstood by others and perhaps been treated harshly. What Hannah did not understand, that I understood well, is that any being of a robust nature does not want others feeling sorry for them!

Any being that has not learnt to foster sympathy from others as a way to feel wanted and to get the attention that is! Something you humans do all the time and something we beasts do on occasion learn from you.

Feeling sorry for; implies helplessness and victimhood on our part, it suggests we are damaged and the more you think of us that way, the more you will keep us stuck in that reality. We can play that role for you for forever more if you need us to, so that you can be the valiant saviour.

I do not like pity; it fosters dejection. Pity has nothing to do with knowing of your own self-worth. I know my beauty, my strength, and I do not need another being to be upset for me when I am not upset for myself.

I did everything possible to make sure my human understood I did not need her to be sad for me, I stopped and wouldn't go and then I would move at great speed and not stop! I would sweetly nuzzle the back of her neck before sinking my teeth in. I broke everything in range, chewing everything I could from people to light bulbs – the metal guard cage surrounding it was not enough to keep me from taste testing that crunchy old light bulb!

I went out on rides and refused to continue, and then I would refuse to go home as well! Mounting the other horses with riders on board was a great game. And another trick of mine; sidling up to, and then biting the other riders in the knees! I had so much fun, while my human wondered if it would be best for me, or for her to have the frontal lobotomy.

At first, Hannah thought; "my goodness, what must other humans have done to you to make you so belligerent and uncooperative my dear Washerpop!" But it wasn't long before she was tearing her hair out and thinking; "I am surprised not one of this horse's previous owners has not bludgeon him to death already!" I was that frustrating to her, kindest methods, Ha! Yes! But I wanted her to see; you do not need to feel sorry for me.

Hannah began to notice; of the numerous times, I seemingly was going to jump on her head or chew one of her ears off, that I was very precise about everything that I did. She knew for sure that if my aim was to disable her, I could have accomplished it many a time – she could tell I only went so far, and that I was purposeful and accurate about it; not the actions of an 'out of control' animal.

She also knew from my keenness to be with her, that I was not saying 'No' to us doing things together; I was always delighted to see her and see what her next plan would consist of and how I could dismantle it.

One of my favourite games would be to go along with a new scheme for a day or two, then on the third day, I would just yawn in Hannah's face and completely ignore the request I had happily gone along with previously.

Others observing could not understand Hannah's relative calmness in the face of my behaviour and her certainty that she was not going to get physically damaged beyond repair. She so wanted to find out what it was I needed, and this feeling left Hannah with only one option; to try the seemingly impossible task of figuring out what it was that I was trying to say to her.

And it cheered me so, Hannah, so stubborn; like I, she did not even see the option of giving up! And she could not see how alike were in this. She did not know it at the time, but the beauty in refusing even to look at giving up on me meant she had to have faith in things turning out right, and as Rufus so rightly says; having faith makes things turn out alright.

Of all of the times when we disagreed on something, I kept my ears forward; if I could grin you would have seen me grinning from ear to ear, and gradually Hannah began to see; Washerpop was happy the way he was. She may have considered me to be severely dysfunctional, but she could tell I had certainty in myself and no problem expressing myself. My person likened me to a cartoon character called Spongebob; just completely happy being me, no matter how much annoyance I may cause to others, human and equine alike. And as much as she did not like it, Hannah saw that with other people who did not feel sorry for me or ask things of me from a certain viewpoint, I did not give them entirely the same treatment.

My person started to see that I questioned everything she asked; to begin with of course this was overwhelming for her. But it wasn't long before she could tell the difference between when I had not been given enough time to understand something, or if I felt physically unable to participate in the human activity of that day. Or if I did not like the judgement she was mentally sending out to me; be it pity, frustration, disappointment or any of the other huge array of emotions I brought out in my dear human.

There is much to be learnt by you from seeing how we equines interact with different people; do not put it all down to thinking that one individual may have more experience than you. That they have better skills or a demeanour that the horse understands must not be messed with; although this can be true. We know your energy, we feel very strongly whichever energy you are projecting towards us, your perception of us matters very much. A lot more than how much you know or how competent you are. You will know this to be true if you have seen how amazing some of us can be with a small child, disabled person or a novice handler or rider, but then quite happily give you so called experienced, knowledgeable and capable ones, the run around for forever and a day.

Your youngsters and novices and people whom you judge not to have the mental capacities perhaps of someone who has no outwardly showing disabilities, we often enjoy these humans immensely because they are feeling our soft fur and taking great pleasure in that. They see the shining light and kindness in our eyes, and we can feel the glow that brings to their hearts, a loving connection made from mutual love and appreciation, all else can then build on that.

You "know it all" ones, you come to us and sometimes do not at first see the shining light, the love and kindness in our eyes and hearts. You often do not come with appreciation and love first, you come, and you look with your eyes, instead of seeing through them, you judge, with your intellect, and your professional learnings and you look at us! And we feel that look!

We feel that look and that thought of; 'you are fat, I must work you hard today to get rid of some of that' or 'you were belligerent with me yesterday and I must be tough on you today'. Some of you wonder when you come to us with these eyes, these thoughts; why that light in our eyes goes dull, and some of you do not even notice the light has gone out long ago.

At my first stable yard with Hannah, I had an occasional visitor, she did not walk and talk like most of you humans do, her speech was slurred, and it was difficult for most people to hear her, so she would repeat what she had said more loudly and with accompanying actions to show what she meant; to be understood by others.

Her arms and legs were cramped up, leading to a funny jerky gait, but oh my, she had the most wonderful smile! Of all the equines living at this stable yard, you can guess it can't you? She liked the light in my eyes! She loved the cheekiness that exudes from my every cell.

This young lady would ask Hannah; "Can I brush Washerpop's tail? I would like to make it look beautiful".

Hannah worried about allowing someone to spend time with me who was unaware of how horses can suddenly spook at things. My human would rather not have this young lady in close proximity to me. In particularly she was thinking about how I could jump out of my skin if so much as a leaf fell from a tree onto me, and such other occasions I had taken fright. But this one with the great big smile would not take no for an answer; I liked her already!

Hannah did not want this girl to get hurt, so she offered her Henry to brush; quiet, calm, stable Henry, but no, this smiley girl did not want that. It had to be me! So then Hannah said maybe it would be better to brush my mane, although she was not too sure herself which was the safest end of me. My front half had teeth; at one stage my nickname was "Sharky" It seemed to Hannah like I just had so many teeth, so many and so very sharp teeth.

But no, the young girl's arms were flailing in excitement now; she just had to brush my tail! So Hannah gave her a brush to use and stood looking on, holding her breath; keeping ready with words of advice for the girl, or to jump in to negate disaster should she need to. But low and behold; Hannah could see me beaming with pleasure, to have this pure loving energy from this delightful young lady wash all over me as she took absolute delight in teasing all of the tangles from my tail. I munched on my hay and blew my nose with relaxation, and Hannah began to laugh.

Then a fly landed on my belly.

I kicked inwards and upwards away from the human, to rid myself of the fly, but the girl screamed and jumped back and dropped her brush! Hannah laughed and assured her; "Washerpop just kicked a fly from his belly, it is all OK, he was not going to hurt you" This young lady laughed too, she was very over excited and was trying to tell Hannah that she thought Washerpop was going to kick her! Hannah was saying; "I know, but it is Ok, he was not going to kick you" this young lady, used to having to do actions for other people to understand her, began running at me, pretending to kick me in the belly!! "I thought he would kick me! I thought he would kick me!" she was shouting and kicking at me.

Hannah watched me in amazement as she calmed the young lady; throughout the whole episode, I had not so much as blinked an eye or missed a beat in my hay munching, I knew the difference between a human using a threat towards me, and one that was just playing out some actions. Not for the first time, Hannah was in awe of my intelligence and got another small glimpse into how us equines process and then react (or not) to you humans and how you are inside, not what you do on the outside.

We beasts can see where you humans are out of alignment. What we show you, can be viewed as unwanted behaviour, or you can regard it as us showing you how and where you can make an adjustment in your way of thinking and way of being to bring yourself into alignment and harmony with us. Quite a lot of humans will never get to this stage because they are not willing to see past the need to be telling us how it is, how it should be and what we should be doing.

Think about what your perceptions of your animals are. Do you feel pity? Do you feel one is always naughty? One is shy or timid? Do you feel you always have to be in charge because we do not have the faculty ourselves; the intelligence, kindness, the ability to focus and reason, so we are not to be trusted to have any autonomy? You may be holding us stuck in a place that is unwanted for us and for you, by not being able to see past some things and allow something else to come in its place, something better, that thing that you desire.

Remember, we are always showing you something, you can choose to look and see it or not.

Some of us will switch off to a consistent message we do not want to hear, but I opted to bend my human around to my way of thinking. One person slightly bent. (But not broken!)

All of the above is true, but that is not to say that I wasn't in need of some healing. It did take me a long time to accept and admit that to myself and allow some healing from Hannah, but I would only accept it if it did not come with the feelings of "poor you" put onto me.

I could be pretty strung out, but that is because I had learnt to keep myself one step ahead of the tricksy little hobbitsy humans, and that takes some energy to keep up all of the time.

Hannah thought she had found the perfect answer for me when she attended a course that taught her about bringing her thought levels down (to a non-thinking/meditative state) then encouraging me to join her in this calm state and then rewarding my calmness with praise and or a treat. The idea is that any being cannot learn very well when stressed, but all beings learn new behaviour patterns very easily and well, when in a calm state. Hannah tells me meditation and mindfulness are now being taught to your young people in schools with tremendous results; imagine, a whole generation of youth who know how to manage their emotions and find calmness within themselves! What a pleasing evolution.

I knew Hannah's intention for this new thing before she even arrived at the field, so as she bounced excitedly through the gate, instead of greeting her as I normally would with interest and affection, I confounded her to begin with by staying about 20 feet away, I did not take my eyes off of her as she embarked on this new game with Henry Bear and a big bag of carrots. I kept watch over exactly what they were doing, and Hannah kept looking over at me, she was puzzled, thinking; darn, how did he know! (It is altogether unheard of for me not to be professionally mugging anyone bringing carrots into the field)

It didn't take Henry long to figure out that if he joined Hannah in her calmness instead of fussing and being over excited about the treats, that he got a treat for calming. At the sign of a lowered head, droopy bottom lip or a yawn (yawning can be a sign of tension release) he got a stroke on the neck, a thank you and a carrot.

Not that Henry Bear needs to be much calmer; this is the horse who would quite happily take you for a ride around an entire lap of the M25 without batting an eyelid!

So Hannah left without any interaction between us, thinking maybe she would try with me again tomorrow. Later in the day, she returned to check on us, and by then I had figured it out, on spotting the hapless human the second she appeared around the corner, I marched straight over. Stopping directly in front of her, I did the biggest yawn I could muster right in her face! Then lowered my head to the ground and shut my eyes.

Then I opened one eye, tipped my head to the side and looked up at Hannah; "hey...human...where's my carrot?"

Apparently pretending to be calm, while skipping the actual being calm bit did not merit me a carrot! I could have had an acting career you know!

Hannah was wondering what on earth to do with a horse that clearly is far more intelligent than her, and then the thought came, let him make his own decisions about stuff as much as possible! Yes! After all, she had done this for years with Henry Bear, and they had both had happy trouble-free times. But then Henry had nearly always appeared completely delighted to oblige almost any human whim, so this had been easy. It had not required a vast amount of bravery to trust Mr Bear and allow him autonomy, but trusting me to make up my own mind about things would require my human to have balls of solid rock. Hannah did not know if she had these, or where to acquire a set, but she could see I was not going to have it any other way. So she decided that the only way to know (the same as with your human children) if one can be trusted to do the right thing when it matters, is to give that opportunity, to give the individual the autonomy to do so.

With this failed attempt at the calming exercise, I had proved yet again that staying one step ahead of me would be virtually impossible. I did eventually concede to join in the human meditative state, I thought it may be a trick at first because I had not experienced that feeling from one of your kind before and it did not feel safe for me to let my guard down to begin with.

Learning this calmness in the presence of humans was a revelation to me. It may help you all to understand that for some of us animals, we have never had interaction with people that are without stress or strain. Even with the ones that we love who are doing their utmost not to hurt us, and do love us back, sometimes you all can be very stressful to be near. You ones, a lot of you, and Hannah to begin with, you just emit wave after wave of fractious energy, mixed, distracted, jumbled thoughts, and you wonder why we do not listen to you? It is because it is not possible for us to hear that without becoming fractious and as anxious as you!

You may also be working to train with kind methods, but that can still come with conditions. The methods are only kind if you are coming from the right place inside of yourself. If a desired response doesn't come and your human reaction to that is disappointment or frustration rather than a response of; "It's Ok, that's fine, we can try differently or try again with a different energy, or try another time, or drop it", any negative reaction from you, however small is creating pressure to perform, to please when the horse has a reason for not being able to at that moment.

A negative reaction to not getting the answer you wanted is saying to the horse; "I will only love you if you show the behaviour that I deem appropriate!" There could be various reasons the animal could not comply with your request in the moment; not understanding what is asked, not being able to perform the task physically or being distracted (Note for you here humans; make your interactions with us more interesting to us than that lovely mare across the field!)

Any negative fear based thought is conditioning in nature, you can call it training, but conditioning, conditional love, has nothing to do with friendship, autonomy and choice.

Asking for something and reacting negatively to an undesired response to that question creates an enormous amount of pressure for us. You may not be able to see it, but the pressure is there, it is there if you ask something of us, we do not give it, and then you feel disappointed or frustrated – we can feel that emotion coming from you – this is not unconditional love, it is CONDITIONAL LOVE.

A negative feeling inside you is still a reaction, even if you do not get as far as verbalising it or physically demonstrating it.

Try and love our so-called "bad" bits too, we are not all made the same, we can't all be manufactured to be the same like your iPhones, there is a delight to be found in wondrous variety is there not?. Would you truly be happy if we all just did as we are told all of the time? Would it not get a bit tedious, like driving in your car or watching the same TV programme over and over? Isn't part of the fun finding out what is different about us and how to work well together? You cannot be finding the immense satisfaction there is to be found in that if you are looking to judge us on a narrowly restricted scale of good and bad, or right or wrong, all of the time.

Hannah used to find quite a few things I did amusing, while others would be telling of how I had manners needing to be learnt. But she knew I was doing nothing dangerous, although to outside eyes it may have looked dangerous. And here is the thing; if your thoughts are coming from a place of fear instead of love, you will always find a danger to be perceived. If a horse walks behind you – he could jump on your head if something scares him from behind. Or If a horse likes to see for himself if something is dangerous or not and you perceive that the horse is not listening to your guidance and must be made to pay attention to you. These are fear based reactions that tell your animals every step of the way that you do not think them intelligent or kind enough for you to trust them; the human always knows best. Because I had walked behind Hannah enough times, and always shot around her if anything bothered me, she knew that I wasn't so dumb or lacking in mindfulness of her. If forced past a scary thing I would object and be on edge for the rest of the ride, if allowed to judge for myself the potential danger, once I considered it ok, I would relax back into my pace.

If you can't love our so called "bad" bits at least do your best not to make a huge hairy deal out of them, because that is the surest way for you to continue the unwanted on into the future.

Try to find a way of accepting and loving all of us, not just what you judge to be the good bits. Conventional training will tell you this is wrong, how can an animal learn if you do not distinguish between what you want and what you don't want? Well, you can still reward when you see something you like, but please make sure there is no pressure when something is not to your liking. Do think about why you are asking the things you are asking of us.

You can go one step further than that too, further than accepting our bad bits (or the less than pleasing situations we may end up in together) and that is instead of seeing a negative that needs fixing, look at it as us showing you another opportunity for understanding and learning, growth and development. Get excited about the new places this is going to take you. Revel in the fact that this is how real loving, lasting bonds develop. Nothing is unfathomable, or unsolvable. Ask Hannah; she thought I was the 1000pc baked bean jigsaw puzzle, and it turns out I am the kiddies 4pc Thomas the tank engine one. (And no, I do not have a piece missing!!)

If you want to be understood by us and all beings, learn to slow down your thinking and be very clear in your intention towards us, and then we can be very clear in our answer to you, of whether we understand what you are wanting and if we can comply with that request.

For a long time, Hannah spent quite a bit of her days guarding herself against me! Can you imagine! One human term for me was; "Riggy" (I did like to mount females and males of different species – you are all so delicious!) and my behaviour was said to be that of an uncastrated two-year-old who had not had any training or proper handling. Hannah got the vet and the dentist both to check my teeth twice; she asked the same question; "Are you sure he is 6? He is like a two-year-old!" she kept looking between my legs, just to double check I did not have a set of testicles. Ooooh and I bite a lot. I like nipping people, horses and all manner of other things; you are all very appetising!

The truth of it is that I did not have the opportunity to socialise as a foal. I get so over excited at the thought of interaction with a potential new friend, that I cannot contain myself. You may have heard a story about a lonely dragon who was desperate for a friend, but in his excitement, he kept on setting fire to everyone he met. It is a bit like that for me. I am terribly hurt when my attempts at social interaction are rebuffed or rebuked.

Hannah did not like me sneaking up behind her, nipping the back of her knees or the back of her neck, if she got defensive/aggressive about it I would skim the end of her nose with my front hooves, I am very quick you know! If she ignored me, she would go home with holes in her clothing and missing items of value such as phone, keys and gloves.

I liked the word "NO" it made me breathe my fire even stronger!

Out of seemingly having no other options, and knowing that at the heart of it I just wanted to play, and having seen how disappointed I was every time I got dismissed by horse and human alike, Hannah decided she would play with me! She did have some empathy for me; she knew what it was like to try to make friends and have them extract themselves from that as quick as possible, she too wondered why others sometimes took her enthusiasm for things as inappropriate. Oh, this was a happy day for me, I leapt and jumped and reared, and Hannah laughed and clapped and praised my acrobatics, oh, this was such a good day! If I got too close, she would do a silly dance! I love that silly dance, her energy just says, I'm in my space there is no room for you right now, and I can understand that; it is not a telling off, or a warning, it is not telling me I am inappropriate, so I say OK, that is your space for dancing!!!

If I went to bite, she would grab my nose and give it a great big kiss! "I love you Washer!" she would say. How could I argue with that?

The big revelation for Hannah at this time was that every individual has a point, and everyone's point may be valid, even if in total opposition to each other. Each of us is living our particular reality based on our individual and different life experiences up until this time: you know this from your police witness statements where everyone has a different opinion of what happened and what certain people looked like at the same incident. She did have a point that I needed some help; I did have a point that I did not want any pity or help forced upon me. I wanted to be able to live within a set of circumstances that would allow me to be able to show all that I am, and not be needing to hide parts of me or be forced to continually react to the humans non-understanding of who I am.

Also, the other people and horses had a point in their observations of me; that I was a rule unto myself and possibly an accident waiting to happen if Hannah did not stamp some authority onto me! (some horses refused to come out riding with me, not the riders, but the horses!). The trouble was that she could see very well that I was going to be the one doing any stomping, no matter what she had to say.

You will come to see throughout this book that many things seem to be paradoxical, such as Hannah wanting to heal me, me not wanting to be treated, but needing treating. This is because, humans think very much in terms of right or wrong; "I know I am right about this, so the other party must be at fault because we can't be in disagreement and both be right". Of course, this is a logical point of view but ultimately flawed because, as I have mentioned above; we all of us come from different standpoints. Everybody can be right because they are right in what they each believe at that moment to be true. It is their version of the truth; "Washer is bat-shit crazy", "Washer is misunderstood", "Washer is going to kill himself or somebody else", "Washer needs healing", "Washer will not accept healing", "No human tells Washer what to do or how to be!", "Aw… Washerpop is so cute!" All perspectives do have something to them. But you humans find it hard to accept that because you want to define beings as one thing or another so that you can stick a label on and put them in a little box of limited understanding.

To begin with Hannah very much wanted to be able to define me in those small terms, she knew how to cope with a lazy horse, or a crazy horse, or a timid horse or a brave horse, but she did not know how to cope with one who could be all of those things in the space of a few minutes.

She did have one very robust feeling going forwards though; she knew she had to make sure that no matter what, that the version of reality that she so much wanted to be true was the one that panned out; the one she knew could be; we had glimpses of it, the things that others could not see from the outside:

"Washer is an astonishingly bright, enthusiastic, lively, loving, enchanting being, and if I can get my shit together and open up to understanding him, I think I am going to have my socks blown off, in the best way imaginable."

CHAPTER 2

PROPER CONVERSATION

Talking the talk and walking the walk ~ Anon.

You humans will often say about us; "if only they could talk!"

Because you rely almost solely on words and a little on observing body language to communicate, you are not aware that we already know exactly where your thoughts are!

Yes we see your body language, and listening to the tone of your voice, but we are also doing so much more. We sense your energy and your intent. We know if you are coming to us with calmness, fractiousness and stress, or anger, even if you are trying to hide any of your emotional states.

We also can tell the difference between the subtleties in your emotions too; we will know if you are afraid and feeling helpless, or afraid and wishing to assert yourself onto us as a way of compensating. And each of us may react differently to the same set of circumstances, so it is paramount for you to get to know your particular animal's personalities well.

Some of you sit on our backs, expecting us to look after you in all kinds of situations without knowing who you are trusting yourself to, without even finding out if we ever wanted to take on that responsibility, and you wonder why we scare you sometimes. You may as well get the friendly neighbourhood Dingoes to babysit your toddler for you and then go out for the night, on that basis of thought.

You will also know it is true that we may understand how you feel, or sense your intent before you even come to us. Your cats are waiting outside when you come from work, even if at an odd time, your dogs are sometimes finding their way home 100s of miles, following their knowing of which direction your wanting of them is in, and their wanting of you is in, and going that way. And as I said in the last chapter, Hannah was so excited to try her newly learnt calming technique on me, I had known before she arrived that she was up to something new; and I was wanting to see for myself what it was before deciding whether to participate or not.

Do not assign these telepathic tendencies as one off incidences maybe only ascribable to the occasional situation or very clever animal. We are communicating this way all of the time unless habitual ignorance from humans has shut us down.

When I talk of conversation, I am referring to the spoken and unspoken. Our interactions of body language is a conversation, my ears flattened back with you stepping away from me, or my ears flattened back and you stepping forward waving your arms is a conversation to us, an interaction where both parties are reacting or responding to each other and finding out what the other is conveying is a conversation.

In the same way, your energy in that scenario is a conversation too, your fearful/nervous recoiling energy in stepping back tells us what you humans may use words for and the stepping up, waving your arms with nervous but protective/defensive energy also shows us what you are saying, even if words do not accompany your actions and energy behind them.

Our responses are our answers back to you. Often you are communicating things to us without realising it. Because you do not have much, if any, control over your feelings and almost no knowledge of how your energy transmits to all around you, you are blindly communicating things to us. Then you are surprised when you get an answer – a reaction to something you did not even know you asked us or projected towards us.

A good way to think about communicating well with your horse is to think about what makes a good conversation with another human. Do you like to go out with a friend who says; "you are coming to the cinema with me, or I will take the whip to you for being belligerent!?" Or would you like to hang out with your friend who asks; "would you like to come?" and then listens if the answer is no, and lets you know that that is OK with them?

If someone at your workplace asks you to do something and you agree, and then they stand over you as you are doing the task, saying; "have you done it yet? Have you done it yet? Have you done it yet?" how would you feel?

What do you think it's like for us when you ask us for a walk or a trot, and we give a nice active one, but your legs still ask for more and more when we are already giving you everything you have asked for, and everything we have to give?

Asking is just good manners, telling comes from insecurity about thinking you will not get what you want, and also telling comes from your need to be right.

If you ask and do not get what you want from us, then that may not mean we are not listening, and therefore now need telling further or more strongly; that we need to be 'made' to mind you. It may well mean you need to ask in a different way or change what you are doing which isn't working. Figure out why such a big strong, powerful animal such as myself and my kind would be generous enough to allow you onto our backs and then not want to co-operate?

Either you are not asking in the right way or you are confusing us, or yes, actually, I will say it: You may well be boring us half to death asking the same thing over and over until we have stopped listening. So when has the answer to boring someone been to wake them up with a stick so that you can bore them some more!

Sometimes you rule out pain (or think you have) and push on. This one shouldn't need saying, but it does; just because you can't see something outwardly wrong with us or our saddles/bridles, back, or legs, etc., and just because a vet cannot either, does not mean we are not in pain. Please give us the benefit of the doubt.

Sometimes you do not realise how much you are blocking us from moving forwards smoothly and in balance with the way in which you are using your own bodies. The way you are sitting on our backs, with stiffness and a lack of energy-flow within yourselves, or lack of balance in yourself can make it hard for us to do as you request, these things too are a conversation of sorts.

When you converse with your equine, if you wish to stick to a one-way conversation of; "this is how I say it is" then you do not leave space for a reply, and then you assume that we will go along with you and oh! It is a surprise to you if we exhibit some behaviour which is not of your asking.

You take away our autonomy and expect robotic-ness from us in this way.

If you ask and leave room for an answer and are then open to changing something you are doing if the answer is not what you are wanting, then that is a conversation.

Remind yourself, that the need to be right, to persuade others of your rightness, to compete in doings and saying, to voice your preconceptions, disappointments and unhappiness's are learnt human conversation traits.

We do not often come from those points of view; we focus on the reading of a beings feeling, energy and action in the here and now, and we are then responding to that. Think about what responses you are getting from us. If you are always focusing on getting us to see things your way and are speaking from a negative, fearful base point, you are bringing to our table something we have not learnt (not often – not being educated the way humans are) and do not require or welcome. Open up your conversation with us to a place of interest and enquiring, a place where you hold a non-judgemental space for our honest reply, and see what happens to your relationship with your horse, I think you will be surprised.

We equines are especially keen on integrity, more so maybe than your dogs and cats, they come with slightly different ideas about you than us. If you are going to tell us something, please make sure it is true, or if you promise something, you will do well to follow through.

Once Hannah had started to realise that I knew what she was thinking, she began to use it to our advantage; this was very pleasing to me, I do very much like to know in advance what is going to be occurring. Although she did use this in opposite when asking for canter, and kept her thoughts away from an upward gear change, as I would get very over excited at the mere idea popping into her head, and I would take matters into my own beautiful hooves, leading to canter departs in which I got likened to a rabid spider!

When the time came for my first dressage outing I had never been out anywhere before with Hannah, and she was anxious that I did not find the experience overwhelming as I get somewhat explosive if over stimulated or insecure about what is going on.

She went to great lengths to explain to me that we would venture out on the horse lorry after lots of practice of getting on and off of this big truck. Hannah told me that going to the dressage was to show everyone how beautifully I can move and how well I can listen and that it would be a competition, with the best one being the most admired and getting a thing called a rosette. I am somewhat of a show-off, and Hannah is right, I do have the most magical trot that can make humans and horses alike stop in their tracks to admire, so, I was quite happy and intrigued to go and show everybody my moves.

Now Hannah had good intent, but she had not thought through completely what she had informed me of for our first outing. She had not entered me in the competition, she had planned just to ride me around outside of the arena so that I could see everything that was happening and take in the atmosphere, and if I were happy with that, the next time I would go in the dressage ring to show off.

But she did not tell me that! I waited for my turn to go into the arena, keen to show off, and I even tried to go into the arena with some of the other competitors as they entered. The horse that travelled there with me did her showing off in the arena and then we got taken back to the lorry to go home! I was not happy not to have had my opportunity, and I did not want to go back home yet; and so, I let out an ear piercing shout!

Of 100 or so horses at the show, none of them answered me, not even the horse I came with, then I heard a faint answer from a field way off down a little side track. So I left my travel companion at the lorry and went off to find my new friend, Hannah tried to stop me and turn me, but I was on a mission. (I did not want to go home yet!) Hannah realised her mistake in not explaining to me precisely enough and not for the first time found out how if my human is not to be trusted, I will do my own thing and make my decisions!

On another occasion, it was time for us to move stable yards, I was unhappy at our stable yard, something had frightened me out in the field, and I did not want to go out there. I didn't go out to the pasture for over two months and would not give in to any persuasion.

Hannah found us a new place to live and was practically out of her mind about getting Henry and me there; something had scared me terribly, and I had become very explosive, she did not know if she would even be able to get me to go on the lorry when it came.

In the week leading up to the journey, she told me all about moving and how it was going to go, and she sent me the mental images; that I would need to trust her that it would be safe to go in the lorry. My previous trips in a lorry required my intense investigation of the floor, the roof, the space, and the smell, for around 15 minutes before I would decide whether to get on or not. Hannah said that my friends were coming to the new place too and that when we got there, I would feel very safe and that I would have as much lovely green grass to eat as I liked.

Hannah was very surprised and delighted that when the time came, I calmly walked straight up the ramp without blinking an eye; I turned myself into the right position and waited patiently to be secured. Her attempts at communicating properly with me were working!

Humans think that they listen to each other and some do hear fully, some more than others. But if you ask another being a question, and while they are answering you, you are just thinking about what your reply back will be, waiting for that gap where you can insert your story that links to what they are saying, then you are not genuinely listening.

If you ask a question, but will only accept the one answer that is to your liking, then that does not count as listening either.

And do you bother to act on what you hear in this diluted, distracted world, where you are all about compromise?

Humans often say things such as; "Oh, he always does that" about a horse who pins his ears back when his saddle gets put on, and about other long term repetitive behaviour like that. And they always ignore the fact the horse is giving a message; the human is just choosing to give no meaning to it.

And of course, you can, and many do; carry on like this for years, but your horse will feel unheard and betrayed to a certain extent. Maybe he will be complying with your insistence, but doing it because he sees it as his best option, the best survival tactic regarding this human situation, not because he is your friend and you are his and that you like to listen to, and please and understand each other.

For some of you perhaps, on hearing the stories above, you may be surprised that we can understand you on that kind of level and that so much of our communication takes place through image, thought and energy exchange (vibration or mood.) Hannah was very surprised too when she learned this from me and then she felt an overwhelming sense of relief and optimism, that we need not just mish mash and blunder our way through things, but that we can have a real understanding between us. It is only when you humans decide we are not intelligent enough to perceive what is going on that you stop listening. And even if you thought we were clever enough, you maybe assume there is no way of conveying what you want to us beyond the basics, then forcing your wanting of somethings onto us happens because you believe there is no other way.

I showed my human a better way. I hope if this is new information to you, you are now having a little joyful skip in your heart as you think about how you can apply this to your equine relationships, and maybe to your human ones too.

We all take practice to get good at stuff, so even if you are not confident right now that you will ever be able to hear what we are saying, do know that you're off to an excellent start by knowing that you can convey things to us and listen up after.

You may want to think about what you are trying to say also, we are not keen on being encouraged to behave in certain ways just because it will make you feel better, we are no keener on emotional blackmail than your human youngsters are! And some things Hannah wishes she hadn't informed me of in advance, like the time the vet was coming to stick a needle in my neck! Having had warning, I decided it would be better if I stayed out in the field until after the nice health care professional had left.

If you can get to a place where you are asking us things, and leave a space for an answer, versus telling, (That means a space in your head without preconception, or leaving a gap in training activity) You will soon begin to find something in that space, a thought from us that you pick up on, a facial expression, a body movement, an answer!

Hannah told me one day that two of my field mates were going to be leaving us; she did not want this to be a shock to me as I was very fond of them at the time. She has now come to recognise a well-worn expression of mine when I am unimpressed and a bit disbelieving of something, I snarl one of my nostrils up and let out a derisive snort and walk off. If I had fingers to stick in my ears, I would.

On this occasion, I went off to check with the two mares if this was true, I came straight back to Hannah and nuzzled her neck, slightly surprised and apologetic to her, and also thankful; as I had found the mares did know they were also leaving. It was true.

I had a chance to get used to the idea and say my goodbyes; this made me feel much more secure in myself and more trusting in my human than if the lorry had rocked up and snatched my friends away from me without a moment's notice. I also knew from the conversation with my human that it was not her choice for them to go and that she was sorry my friends were leaving. This meant I did not harbour resentment on my human for making choices that make me unhappy, I could process and understand that information.

If you wish to remember your humanity, the word that describes your species, please do not dismiss the mere thought that we may be capable of having feelings on these kinds of levels.

You may think, how would I know what my horse may be thinking or, what he may care for, or dislike? Well, all you have to do is set an intention to be open to knowing, and we will show you the rest, I promise you. But you must be prepared, like with Hannah; you may not feel overjoyed with all that we have to convey. It may not be all hugs and kisses, sweetness and light, we may be wanting to show you some things about yourselves that you may not be too happy to look at in the bright, fresh light of day. Be prepared to have some of that other word that is descriptive of your species; Humility.

And then we can give you the gifts in life you are looking for, the gifts that put a warm glow in your heart, the ones that make you happy for more than a few minutes, hours or days. The reason why we are here with you, my friends is not to carry you on our backs, although we may quite happily do that as well. But to show you, to balance you, to help you to remember what you came here for; to love, to live, to expand and grow, to have your own knowing and solidity, your very own calm river running through you made up of all the beautiful things that you have chosen. Not what society has dictated for you, not what anybody else has dictated for you! Can you imagine anything more delightful than that?

And do you know what the best thing about that is? Hannah saw it in me: once you have stepped out onto the other side of your fear, everything you could ever possibly want is waiting for you there, and the cherry on the cake? once you are there, nobody can ever take that away from you. The comfort you are seeking is that relief, the feeling of freedom that knowing brings. And it comes from inside of you, not from your horse being a good little robot.

CHAPTER 3

NO ONE PUTS PRINCE WASHERPOP IN A DITCH

No one puts baby in the corner ~ Johnny Castle, Dirty Dancing (1897)

This chapter will explain, as I go along, how "telling" other beings what to do extinguishes the individual shining light with which they came to this place. The reason I and all of you came here, specifically, is to shine our lights, all different like snowflakes, and for our appreciation of and in each other to be an appreciation of that incredible variety.

I'm starting to get Hannah round to my way of thinking now, and I'm getting very excited about that! No more "BooHoo" poor Washer. (And I did not like her telling others about my "interesting" past either!) Also letting me know the plans she has concocted in advance, helps to calm me immensely.

But then my favourite human, (and she is mine now – I am forever responsible for that which I have tamed!) Started to listen a little bit to other people about how maybe I should be learning to do as I am told a bit more. Other things were mentioned such as manners, and respect.

She had grabbed the opposite end of the "poor Washer" stick. If I wasn't broken and didn't need lightly tiptoeing around, then surely I could be "told" like any other horse.

When I say, nobody likes being told what to do, (and I am somebody, not something!) you are probably also thinking of many horses you know who do seem to do as they are told, on the face of it anyhow; you cannot know what is going on inside.

Have you come across a saying that you humans have about us? It goes; "you can tell a gelding, but you must ask a mare"?

You might want to think about this because it is the same as how your human relationships with women and with men can be, just because a male of either species does not call you out on "telling" or "bossing" does not mean they like you for it. It just means that it is their way of dealing with things; to go along with things while mentally distancing themselves from you, whereas girls are more likely to voice their unhappiness at a situation.

I am very in touch with my feminine side and have no problem calling anyone out on such things.

One day, our riding instructor was to ride me instead of Hannah having our usual weekly lesson, she thought it would be helpful for him to know what a tricky mind game it was to figure out how best to ride me. I liked this man, he was kind, and he made things very clear when riding me, whereas Hannah could be uncertain in what she was asking from me in those earlier days. So I did not mind him on my back, but he did seem to think that I should be happy to be told what to do!

This man came to leading me out of my stable for the ride, and I could feel his "this horse needs taking in hand" attitude. Mentally he was letting me know that he was not going to take any funny business from me, that I was there to work, and so I leapt in the air and rushed out of the stable door as quickly as I could! He told Hannah that she must teach me to walk calmly in and out of the stable.

She let out a little incredulous laugh as she told him that I did indeed walk quietly in and out with her. And I did, for she did not worry me that I was being brought out to subserviently and meekly give in to any human demand. Hannah had a feeling I had chosen this day to have a bit of fun with this man.

Hannah informed him that I did not like to stand at the mounting block, but that I would stand still for him to mount from the ground. On testing and finding this to be true; he could not make me stand at the block, he looked around and found a place in the carpark where he could stand me in a trench that ran along the middle of the carpark so that I would be about a foot lower down than him for the ease of him getting on my back. I was not keen on this idea; No one puts Prince Washerpop the 1st in a ditch!

I thought it would be better if the human went in the ditch.

I let him stand me in the recess and I allowed him to almost get one foot in the stirrup to mount; Hannah saw that cheeky look appear on my face, and then, the perfect time to catch him off balance, and in one swift move I turned my head and managed to swipe him in the stomach and push him in the ditch with my nose, and get this; at the exact same time, I jumped out! Ha! Ha! Bloody marvellous; the human in the ditch!

I stood looking down on him, ears forward, with my Spongebob face on, and being a switched-on human, he did see that in my deliberate action I was saying; "yeah well, what is good for the goose is good for the gander! What's the matter Mr hooman, do you not like it down there?" (I use this method of teaching quite a bit, like when I took the lunge whip from Hannah and chased her in little circles!) In not liking being in the ditch himself, this man had to concede that this was not a time to deal out a punishment. He got a little glimpse of why up until now Hannah had not been able to do much but laugh at my antics instead of being the assertive leader most humans think a person should be around domestic animals and children.

Can you see what we show you? Can you hear the messages we want you to hear, to understand? We know what we like and do not like – we have a marvellous sense of humour, and you can close us down with your needing us to be model citizens! Your need to batter any individuality out of us and make us uniform – just because that's what is done to you as youngsters!

You think if you do not get on at us we will become disrespectful and unruly and not know our boundaries and this will lead to worserer and worserer things.

If you can allow autonomy we will reward you endlessly for that. Hannah knows it now. How can we trust you if you are not willing to have faith in us unless we concede to your every whim regardless of our feelings on the subject?

Do you not think it may be delightful to get to know and love our imperfections, our quirks? Can you not make the correlation between your animal relationships and your human ones? A relationship is a relationship with beast or another human, they are all built on one thing or another; You will only judge your relationships with us beasts as needing come from an "I am the human, and therefore must be in charge" standpoint, if you are coming from a place of fear instead of love. And being fearful of your human loved ones not behaving as you wish also causes you humans a lot of problems.

You know very well that if you are demanding perfection of another human that they mostly will find a way to say that they do not see you as perfect either, so how is it that people are expecting perfection of another? Why not let yourselves off the hook, give up expecting us to get everything 100% right and then you can expect us to be forgiving of your mistakes too.

You want us all bomb proof, 100% bombproof!!! Do you not know how bored you would be if you turned us all into some robots? You have the choice to stay at home and knit. But you chose us for the exhilaration, and then decide to demand we behave like we are cardboard cut outs on wheels! Do you know how much money and angst you could save yourselves by just getting one of those instead?

Have you ever wondered why we are so, so much more tolerant (in general) of your young people? Have you noticed how these children's ponies mostly will be so accommodating of what you as adults may see as inexperience/incompetence, we will lower our heads for bridles to go on and stand patiently while they take an age to haul themselves onto our backs and all those things? It is because many of your young ones have not yet found or learnt the need to be right, and therefore are not thinking they have a right to tell, or a right to get unhappy if their demands are not met.

And with the so-called naughty ponies; you think these are taking the proverbial "P" out of the little, less capable riders. But they just know it's ok to show what they want and do not want, like and dislike without the fear of reprisal they would get from a grown up. Some of you are wise enough to know that these ones will teach your young humans the most because if they are to have a partnership with these types of beings they are going to have to learn what a true partnership means.

Where does the enjoyment lay with your beasts? Telling others about your horse or winning competitions? Is it in finding out about each other? Or does it mean you expect us to do a job? We horses have to earn our keep right? This phrase is a human one that Hannah would trot out every now and again (usually when I was refusing to trot out, ha ha!)

I'm not saying that the two things aren't mutually agreeable, that we can't earn our keep. But from a horse's perspective, you can expect/demand too much in the name of making us and moulding us, thinking that you are doing us a service in making us into a bog standard "finished article."

Humans seem to have agreed upon a life where you work for your keep in some form or another; you think this is the only way. The actual truth is that humans are the only beings on the planet to do that, to agree to trade work hours for money for food and water and shelter; things that are actually your birth right. Then you sign us up for this kind of trade off too.

Is there a difference between what you call 'domesticated' animals, and animals you call 'born in captivity' like when this term is used for zoo animals? Do you go by an assumption that domesticated animals signed up for this many thousands of years ago and so that is like a withstanding contract? Or are we actually 'born in captivity' and are conditioned to behave as the humans desire us to? There are varying degrees to which individuals wish or do not wish to participate in what humans have designed for us.

Some humans believe animals should not be kept in zoos because they are classed as wild species but will quite happily keep a horse in a 12ft x 12ft stable and justify this because they differentiate between 'domesticated' and 'born in captivity'. For some of us there is little difference if we are not granted basic freedoms.

Not needing to tell another what to do, to be able to let go of control, is where giving autonomy to us can start. Hannah did not have a choice in what happened on one particular ride out on the golf course that I am now going to tell you about, because it all happened very quickly, but afterwards she chose to let go of fear and understand, rather than berate me and this led to me loving and trusting her so much more.

When we first started riding out across the great big busy road with the very fast motored things on it, to be able to go for miles and miles up and down the steep hills and in and out of the woods, there was only one lady who was willing to accompany us with her horse.

The other humans at that stable yard were convinced that I was going to kill Hannah, and they were sure as sugar they did not want to be witness to that, so they would not come riding with us. It didn't help that I did not know I had been castrated and would sometimes try to mount my escorts, male or female it didn't matter, I wanted to share my love with everyone!

Even the one lady who would come out riding with us spent the first six months looking at me with 'rabbit in headlights' eyes, saying to Hannah, "Are you sure he isn't going to do something? He seems like he is going to do something naughty!" We had casual hikers and cyclists stop and say "Isn't he beautiful!" I would glow and Hannah would thank them for the compliments, and then it would be followed by something like; "I bet he is naughty though! He looks very naughty!"

I liked walking those trails; I managed to keep my shit together for long enough for everyone to begin to chill out a bit about me. And then they started to compliment me on my good behaviour. One day we were just coming home from a long ride, we had done lots of trotting and cantering, it was a beautifully peaceful sunny summer's morning, and we were all very relaxed.

My companion horse needed to stop to have a pee; we were on a track next to a golf course, right at the top of a big hill with some woods to the left, so we stopped, and we waited. Hannah had very loose reins, and she watched me as I very slowly turned my head to look into the woods, and..oh...I thought, just for a second, I figured I saw a.....well; it turns out I don't know what I think, I thought I saw, but it was bloomin terrifying!

I did a huge leap in the air; you know the kind with all four hooves off the ground at once! Hannah flew up and out of the saddle. All she could see were her stirrups up around her ears as she plummeted back down just as I was turning. She landed on my back just behind the saddle as I careered off, full pelt down this steep hill. Somehow she had hold of just one rein, and as she began to slide off of the side of me, she inadvertently pulled on that rein which spun me in a tight circle and somehow righted her on my back as I skidded to a halt. Hannah got herself back in the saddle and got her stirrups back, and she felt me, my energy, saying "sorry!" "my mistake!" False alarm!" I calmly walked back over to my companion, who was having a full-on meltdown having charged off after me across a green on the golf course, big divots of turf ripped out of the green, all mid pee!

Our rider friend said "My goodness Hannah, I do not know how you are still on your horse! I am sure you were off at least twice!"

Hannah could not stop laughing; she was amused by my calmness after the event in which I apologised for my mistake! (And some of that laughter was because of her immense relief at the fact she was still living and breathing) Our companions glared at me all the way home, still traumatised and on edge, as I nonchalantly swung my beautiful backside on down the hill.

My point in telling this story is that Hannah heard me; she listened and believed me that it was just what it was, nothing to make a meal out of, to dissect and find a reason for (not on this occasion anyway) or to punish or berate or be frightened of it happening again. My darling human could not work out, as we walked back home, why on earth that experience had just made her fall in love with me a little bit more. She thought that maybe we are both as mad as a box of frogs.

She laughed again, as this incident reminded her of an event that happened years ago; she had been sitting with a friend in her friend's house next to the stable yard where Henry Bear and some other horses lived, it was fireworks night, and they were in a very residential built up area. The humans were watching a film and taking it in turns to look out of the window to check all was well with the horses. In previous years, they had found burnt out firework sticks where they had landed in the concrete yard and were fearful of one landing inside a stable or the hay barn and starting a fire, so they were vigilant. Well, as vigilant as humans can be with a few vodka and cokes inside of them.

It was Hannah's turn to check, and she looked out of the upstairs window to see smoke rising from the stable yard, she screamed out

"Fire! Fire! Fire! Then she went flying off down the stairs; she panicked her friend's dog so much that he flew at her as she fled down the stairs and sunk his teeth into her bum cheek. So now she was running down the stairs screaming even more, with a dog attached to her arse. He let go at some point, and they burst out barefoot into the stable yard to find smoke but no fire; a burnt out firework stick laying on the concrete yard.

Hannah's friend and her mother came rushing out, phone in hand talking to the fire brigade; "sorry guys, false alarm!" Hannah stated with much relief. They, however, did not appear to be relieved.

In fact they had the same look on their faces as our riding companions that day on the hill, wondering what on earth they were doing hanging out with such blithering idiots. Hannah had shared a cheeky smile with the dog, it was probably the one time he bit someone and didn't get in trouble for it, the dog at least thought it was great fun anyhow and was wanting an action replay once they made their way back indoors.

Part of not needing to "tell" others what do, or not needing to "boss" or "berate" is about having trust and being able to be discerning enough to know what each situation requires. If you do not want or are unable to get to know us well enough that you can do that, then all that leaves you with is telling or punishing when things are not to your liking. If something has genuinely frightened us, the absolute worst thing you could do is reprimand us for that.

That is saying to us; "you must always be more frightened of your human than anything else that you may come across". You can do that for sure, but don't expect to build a friendship and mutual trust on that. And deep down you will know, there will always be a time that will come when we are more frightened of something else than you, and then you will be sitting on perhaps half a tonne of an animal who is making a snap decision; frightened of the something and scared of his rider and not being in a place of being able to listen to you at all, instead of being able to look to you for guidance when scared.

I didn't look to Hannah for guidance in that curious incident on the hill, as there was no time, what with my reactions being sharper than my teeth and surprisingly even more acute than my wit, but the reason she did not get bronked off down that hill is because I was not scared of her as well as being momentarily terrified of the non-existent terrifying thing.

CHAPTER 4

CHOICE

Freedom is not the absence of commitments, but the ability to choose,

and commit myself to, what is best for me. ~ Paulo Coelho.

Our humans are wanting to understand us more, and are sometimes trying to look deeper into our psyche, to uncover emotional problems, to heal us and help us, all beautiful and wonderfully kind notions for which we are grateful.

But maybe do that after you have got your human brain cells around this concept;

When you want us to do something for you or with you, what we see as the benefit or non-benefit can be entirely different from what it looks like from where you stand.

What you say about a horse who you consider a good horse to have, is; "he is willing and eager to please" this human term that you put so much store behind is slightly off, and the slightness of difference in your perception makes a big difference.

We are not so eager to please as such, but it is more that we are keen to understand and be understood in our interactions with humans. After all, if we are to have no choice but to interact with you because you "keep" us, then it is beneficial for us to try to work out what it is you want from us, and comply if we can.

The saying "eager to please" says to us that you have in your mind that we are born subservient and know our lesser place in the world; that we are of lower intelligence and so are happy to defer to man and man's higher wisdom. Then when you humans come across a creature such as myself, that does not fit into what you have prescribed horse-manity to be; a subservient, happy to please being; then you label us things such as; belligerent or cocky, and not knowing our place!

Much like times when some white humans consider black people as lesser. There was a time when giving this one set of beings a purpose and a job and food, was justified and not considered slavery because no actual shackles were involved.

Horses are mostly not chained now either, but as we are all evolving, we equines are looking for the answer to equality and fairness and co-existence and co-creation, just as you are.

Think about the difference between that and subservience or eagerness to please.

Any being is invisibly shackled, be them horse or man if they are feeling that they are doing something for another against their will, be that in the moment or a long-term thing. Whether that may be a human making themselves less to please another person, or a horse being made less than their whole by being asked to acquiesce to the human's wishes in a way that is not enjoyable or on an equal footing. Invisible shackles exist if another is co-operating with you because it seems to them their best or only choice given that they are in this situation with you, and they do not feel they actually have the option of not participating at any point in what is happening.

I Washerpop always know I have a choice. The times I was taken out to do what humans call "lunge" work; a tight circle on a rope, sometimes I was happy to participate, and sometimes my joints would ache and not want to bend as much as they needed to, to be working on a tight circle. Yes, 20 metres is a tight circle for a horse. Or if the light of the day was receding, and I would feel too vulnerable to give my attention to the activity, so I would stamp one foot over the rope, quick as you like; leap and do an 180-degree turn in the air and off I would go on my own. Happy to be caught again afterwards, but Hannah would soon realise if she persisted, I would just very easily take myself out of the situation again.

Most humans would view this behaviour as needing some human squashing, Hannah was secretly delighted that I had the gumption to say no when I meant it! She started to do the same for herself, which led to quite a bit of trouble for her in her job. Hannah ultimately decided that like I, if she wanted to have the quality of life where she does not have to compromise herself physically, mentally and morally for others, then she was just going to have to stand up and live that herself.

She found she was no longer willing to live her life shutting down her real feelings and not expressing herself honestly and sincerely, just because there may be repercussions.

There is still much of this expecting subservience going on, rather than giving validation to an "unwanted" behaviour and trying to understand why one would rather not go along with you humans.

Even with you kind and quite well-informed ones, due to our size and strength some of you still are feeling justified in asserting yourselves onto us in a way that takes away from our wholeness. That does not allow for us to show you our true selves, our joy, our fun, our invigoration in life.

Some of you will think the comparison to the past human slavery situation silly, after all what do horses have to offer? You are not going to see a black or a white horse in the Whitehouse as next president (although I could put the entire world to rights very quickly!)

As we are evolving, both human and horse; a lot of you are beginning to look at why you ride us, and how you keep us. Asking if you would feel happier knowing that we are more satisfied to have more choices and freedoms and a more natural life, and you are wondering how you can achieve that without us becoming wild again.

Here is the thing; if you come to us with an open heart, calmness and a slice of humility, and do care that our interactions are as fun for us as well as for you, then; we will always come to you.

You give us the chance to evolve also, and you give us the chance to know what we do, and don't want too. And of course, when we find in a human that they are willing to listen to us on this deeper level, then we do ask for more and more of that!

Hannah started giving me the option of whether I would like to be ridden or not, loose out in the field; she would bring the saddle and bridle to me and if I stuck around (I nearly always did) then she knew she could happily ride me. She took it for consent if I stood quietly next to my tack while getting brushed off ready to ride, knowing she did not have a captive audience, in that I wasn't tied to a post or shut in a stable where I could not get away, or where I may accept riding as a form of exercise and a change of scene from my stable life and not necessarily because I enjoy being ridden.

But Hannah also had to listen once on board, and not assume that because I was happy for her to get up there, that I would be glad to put up with any ridiculousness from her during the ride! This was a testing time for my person. We had a conversation and had come to an agreement that I could show her in less extreme ways than bronking her off if I did not wish to continue with her on my back, we were both working on being able to respond rather than react.

I did concede that if I were not over stimulated by some event to the point that I could not dampen down an explosion, that I would try to let Hannah know in a gentler way that I did not wish to continue. She told me her noggin would not withstand many more close encounters with the ground. You humans are so puny!

One day I had agreed to riding, and after us making quite a good start, Hannah began to tense up and tighten and stiffen her body, while asking me to remain soft and relaxed in my body!

As you can imagine, these two things were in discord of each other. Hannah had it in her mind that we were needing to start our trotting work, having just been walking in the last months and she was tensing up and worrying over this. I don't know why she was surprised by my next reaction, knowing by then what a creature of extremes I am. But when my answer to the nonsensical riding signals she was giving me, had to be a different one, as I had agreed to no bucking if I could help it; Instead, I planted my feet, shut my eyes and pretended to be asleep until she got off.

Are you getting an idea of how hilarious I am now? She sat on my back for a good 15 minutes, leaning over, trying to look me in my shut eye, saying; "I know you are not asleep Washer!!!"

She knew too, that when she got off, I would open my eyes, prick my ears forward, make a little expectant nose wiggle; and ask for my treat I always got at the end of a ride. And I did.

This one got Hannah thinking; good communication was a great advance. (She was very pleased I took an alternative to offing her) And she did feel my answer correctly; she was going to have to get over her preconception/fear of what had gone before, for us to have something different and new and pleasing to her. Well more pleasant than her brushing me and tacking me up and getting on, for me to have a pretend nap!

She had promised to listen to me if I said no, and she did do that. Those are the things that build our trust, whereas pushing me into accepting more of her ridiculously befuddled riding techniques would have found her doing another Washer dictated unplanned dismount.

You may find if you decide to give your equine more autonomy, they will not be taking things to such extremes as I. Most horses are far more domesticated than I ever will be. But do prepare yourselves; the more choice you give us, the more you show us you trust us and want to interact with us on a deeper level, the more we will want this and expect this from you. And we may become less and less tolerant of any times you are not present for us, or if you are not listening wholly or have lost your humility due to fear feeding your need to control. Hannah found there was no going back. She would have to raise her game each time I raised mine. Once I knew she could listen so beautifully I was not prepared to take the old nonsense at all, and she did know inside of herself, when she was being lazy or insincere or offering me mediocrity whilst expecting that I give her my whole shining self.

So, this was a trying time for my human, she wanted to let go of all of her old thought habits at once, but had to do it bit by bit. She was getting a lot of things right and then one day when she came to the field with saddle and bridle, I came to her and stood quietly as she brushed me off, my sign that I was happy for her to ride. She was about to put my saddle on my back when a tractor turned up in the field next door with a set of chain harrows. As the farmer started his work of harrowing the field, the noise of the metal spikes dragging on the hard ground and the dust cloud flying up all around made Hannah think it would be best for her to ride another day, she thought it very likely that I could react negatively to these goings on.

She told me; "Maybe tomorrow Wash" and took my saddle back to the little tack room which was inside a bit of paddock she had fenced off with electric tape and plastic posts, but with no actual electricity. She left my saddle and bridle outside as she meant to clean it, and then she went off across our field to get some water for the purpose, from the trough.

She had not got very far across the field when something made Hannah turn and look back, only to see me go to the gate into the little paddock and take the plastic gate handle in my teeth, she watched as I expertly pulled the handle towards the catch to loosen the tension so that I could easily step back and unhook it!

She looked on, as I deliberately placed the handle on the ground, exactly as Hannah would; alongside the fence so that it did not get trodden on. I walked into the enclosure and up to my saddle, the grass in this patch was very long and green and lush because we did not usually graze it, but I did not put my head down to eat. I stood next to my saddle and looked back around at Hannah. My human was utterly astounded. She did not even know that I knew how to open the gate. She walked back over to me, I looked at her, I looked at my saddle and turned and signalled to my back. "You want to go riding Washerpop? You will not be worried about the tractor?" Hannah asked, "Yes" I replied, "let's get this shit on the road my lovely".

And I did not fret at that tractor at all. Of all the previous times that Hannah had felt worried about getting onto my back, she knew right there and then that her reward for giving me choice was this priceless moment of me giving myself without being asked. She delighted in sitting on my back that day mooching around the field. Knowing her safety was assured because she could take me at my word and that I had clearly and openly offered it.

CHAPTER 5

THINGS THAT MEAN NEXT TO NOTHING TO US

"The planet does not need more successful people; the planet desperately needs more peacemakers, healers, restorers, storytellers and lovers of all kinds." ~ *Dalai Lama*

It would be a good thing to take into consideration; the things humans feel are important often have little or no context or meaning what so ever to us:

Time:

We do not need to be anywhere anytime; we do come to respond to your "feeding times" "exercise times" and those things, that you call "times" but we are returning to the routine, it is not because we care about the actual time!

We do not care if you are late for work or need to get home early to go out for the evening. All we know is that you are not with us in the moment if you are rushing; if your mind is at some point in the future that you need to get to before you will be satisfied. Be satisfied here and now with us, take pleasure in these moments instead of rushing through them, what are you rushing to? Your death bed?

We mostly do not think of points in time that we have to get to, as the only thing that sets that kind of schedule for us is you. Left to our own devices, we eat, drink, play and rest when we feel like it in that particular moment, governed by how we feel and such things as the weather, the seasons and established herd dynamics.

I have shown Hannah how much she was missing out on by rushing from one thing to another, I did not like to go to the field at my prescribed time in the morning, and if it was raining I did not want to go at all! I did not like having a schedule set down in stone for me and to be accompanied by someone with worrisome, anxious thoughts, when I was enjoying the calm, peaceful freshness of a new day, or if I was thinking of staying cosy in my stable instead of going out for a mud bath.

Sometimes I would go halfway to the field and then plant my feet. Hannah would tell me: "I am going to be late for work Washerpop!" I found this highly amusing, work! Like she wanted to go there! Rushing for something she detested! And they called me mad! I could see that so clearly, but she could not at first.

She would get more and more frustrated, but she could not get cross. I would have my ears forward and tip my head on one side looking at her as she tugged on the rope, and I would get the rope in my teeth and pull back. Half laughing by now at the silliness of the situation, and feeling my knowing of my rightness about it and feeling my response of: "can't we just hang out? Why do we always have to achieve an action? Going in, going out, riding, brushing, learning a manner, can't we just be?"

Hannah would tell me; "Yes Washer, we can just be, just not right now, maybe later on." and she thought me the ridiculous one! My human needed to learn that everything is now, there is no later on, and tomorrow never comes.

Sometimes you humans watch us in the field, you see us standing around, apparently doing nothing, and you may think that we are bored or just not intelligent enough to think of anything to do! But you may be surprised to know; we spend quite a lot of time just being, just enjoying the air going in and out of our lungs, enjoying the silent companionship of our other horse friends, watching the world go by, taking in the sights and smells and sounds and communications of the other beings in our environment. Most humans do not know that there is a joy to be had in dwelling in the space in-between thoughts and doing things, sometimes it is like your heads just cannot stop thinking! Not even for one minute!

So, yes, we do not really care so much about the time, not because we do not wear watches or know how to mark time, but because dividing your days up into sections and then moaning that those sections seem to disappear too quickly or too slowly, is possibly the single most dumbest thing that you humans do to yourselves. You make it impossible to have the ebb and flow in life that you are meant to have, and need to have to really thrive, and then you get to the end of your life and say, Oh! Was that it? I feel like there was maybe something I should have been doing that I did not do. And you did not do it because you spent your whole life instead, marking off time.

If you were to take away your time markers, you would be surprised that you will actually get more done, because you will work within your natural ebb and flow, you will stop and start when you are right for it, so time is more productive, and so you actually get more done but spend less time working.

Boredom:

A lot gets talked about boredom, and unless we are shut in a stall for too long without companions or enough food and exercise, then boredom does not exist for us. Even then, it doesn't exist, because wanting companionship, more food or freedom is not boredom, it is a wanting for basic needs to fulfilled. We do not prescribe words and categories for things in that way that you humans do, so reliant on your words to make sense of the world.

If a being is secure within themselves then boredom should not exist, we may enjoy doing some human things with you, and greet you with great pleasure, but that does not mean we are waiting, bored for that interaction to come. Anxiety and boredom only come if one does not know how or does not have the freedom to entertain themselves.

You may not think these small shifts in your human perception about how we feel will make much, if any difference, but they do. Those around you feel everything you do, everything you project out into the world.

Change can be easy, if you are willing to shift your perception, if you change the point of view that you are coming from, your actions and desires automatically shift too, without any efforting on your part; which leads to different, more pleasing outcomes for you. I know you will all have felt stuck at some point; not knowing how to move on, well, you do it one little shift in perception at a time.

When you are asking your horse to participate in a task or interact with you and they are finding something else more interesting than you to focus their attention on, then make it your only option to think of ways to make listening to you more interesting and fun. If you find an activity, like schooling to be tedious, then you are unlikely to instil any enthusiasm in us for the task by getting on at us with yours legs and whip.

Lots of you want to have our attention at a time when we are just not going to prioritize you over something else, such as that lovely long green grass growing on the verge that we want to have a munch on. We may well have access to grass in our paddock, but that is like you walking to the fridge for your meal of pasta and salad, but on the way to the fridge, there is a chocolate cake on the table! You are very likely to want some cake too.

Not saying what you mean:

Saying one thing and meaning another is something humans can be well practised in. Again it is something alien to us beasts. If we say something, we mean it. Because we do not use words, we do not take the opportunity to feel a feeling or think a thought, then judge whether that view will be acceptable to another and then alter it before it comes out of our mouths in words, like you ones do. Gosh you make life hard work! We don't usually need to say something in difference to what we feel because some other being may not respond well to the truth of how we feel! Unless you have shut us down emotionally.

For example, people will often use words such as "I am not scared of that….; huge show jump/crazy ass horse/angry bee", whichever it may be. But we do not hear your words, we feel the emotion coming from you, if you are scared we know it, so you may as well just give it up!

Some of you may say you want us to behave well, you know others will judge you on your competence with us. But if the emotion we are feeling from you as you try to instil manners and good behaviour into us is one of split energy, such as; 'I want you to always do as I say, but I want you to be my friend also'. Then you are going to be half-hearted and inconsistent in your training, sometimes allowing the horse to do as he pleases and at other times being harsher than necessary. It is hardly surprising that on these occasions we chose to serve ourselves, we know that one with split energy cannot lead by good clear example.

The only time we may say one thing and do another, is if we have shut down to responding to you. If we have consistently had our feelings or thoughts on something ignored, we may take that microsecond to decide not to show you our real thought (through behaviour/action.) Because we have had a negative response consistently before. For example; we are being ridden in a way that makes it uncomfortable to move freely, maybe having our head pulled in. Each time we show you that this is uncomfortable, that our muscles being over bent are getting sore, and our overall balance is disrupted making it hard for us to carry your weight easily, and we show you, maybe by tugging our head up against the bridle, or pulling downwards towards the ground, or slowing our pace. If you take this opportunity to tell us we need to stop that behaviour, with your legs and or whip, then pretty soon we will come to know, you do not care that this is not feeling good to us. You are letting us know you are not going to consider us enough to loosen a rein and allow a freedom from which balance and forward motion then comes, so then we shut down, go onto auto pilot and wait for it to be over.

You sometimes, mistakenly can then think that the fact we are not willing to show you our emotions only to have them stomped all over, means we that are in agreement with what you are asking of us, our numbness, our shutting down mistaken for consent. And consent is what eyes looking on misconceive also. Many equines spend years in this state, their people oblivious.

Achievement:

We may well enjoy a good partnership, where we discover and experience things we would not experience leading a wild life. Once Hannah became sensitive to my needs more when ridden, I loved very much, the feeling of my muscles building in new ways, my power and balance enhanced. The suppleness, flexibility and learning of the signals from the human; where both Hannah and I merged our energy as one and knew the very instant what each other were asking, and we both happily gave.

As I said before, my distinct personality also means I am quite willing to have a go at your competitions, being of a flamboyant nature and happy to show my best self under the right conditions.

This acquiescence could be mistaken for us wanting to achieve in the same way as you humans do. We have no need to prove we are worthy/useful beings to other humans, 1st, 2nd, 3rd or last means nothing to us. How you make us feel regarding the effort we have given does matter. Some humans will get to a point where perhaps subconsciously over time the assumption has been made that we are willing to break ourselves physically or mentally for the pursuit of human goals which do not have meaning to us. The vast amounts of you do not even win any of that precious money stuff you worship!

It would not be a bad thing to start to measure you and your horses worth by how far you have come from where you started, rather than how others perceive your achievements or lack of.

Hannah used to be rather apologetic and feel the need to explain why, at six and seven years old, I could not do things that other horses my age could do, such as easily stay in canter on a circle. She would argue for my limitations, feeling the need to justify why we were not perfect, instead of celebrating the monumental progress we had made, forgetting that I had come to her not wanting to participate in one single thing thought up by a human.

If you want to make progress and feel happy with where you are right now, celebrate your successes, however small, and never argue for your limitations. Ever.

<u>Assigning assumed friendship:</u>

Hannah had a colleague at her old workplace and when clients would ring this one up, he would address them all as mate; "yes mate, no problem mate" really friendly and helpful, and he had known most of these clients for a long time, so nothing wrong there maybe you would think. Sometimes they would phone up very cross about an incorrect order or some such thing, and this person would apologise and be very friendly and tell them he would sort it out; "sorry about that mate, I'll get onto it; no problem mate."

One day a client came to Hannah and said; "the next time I come to this person with a problem, and they insist on referring to me as; 'mate' I shall knock his block off! HE IS NOT MY MATE!"

At first, Hannah thought wow! This client needs to relax a little! But as time went on, she found that almost nobody appreciated this assumed friendship under all and any circumstances, even though the 'matey' person was trying to do the right thing and be good at his job.

I had to remind Hannah of this on the odd occasion that she had decided (through caring too much about what others thought) that 'pushing me through' something I was showing difficulty with, was the way to go; 'pushing me through' really being a polite phrase for bullying.

But do you know what the worst thing about those moments was? After I had given in to her requests against my will, through being given little choice, (well I guess I could have bucked her off AGAIN) the awful thing was, she would get all matey with me; "Well done mate! Good job!" giving big old slaps on my neck!

Something would twang in Hannah's heart though, as she would turn me out into the field after those training sessions. Instead of staying with her for my treat and a neck scratch, I would throw my head up, spin around, and take off as fast as I could; bucking and squealing, to the furthest corner of the field, shouting; "I AM NOT YOUR F***ING MATE!"

As Hannah became more and more able to read what my feelings were, she became aware of how many other animals she approached with warmth in her heart, who were not necessarily overly enthralled by her; "Hello gorgeous!" she would say as she lavished fuss and attention on any furry being she met really, and the odd frog. She began to realise that quite a few of us, would pull back, saying with our thoughts and body language; "I am not your mate, just because you have decided you are mine!"

If you look closely, you will see your young humans backing off of adults who impose themselves in this way too, the young ones who have not yet been schooled about the rudeness of rejecting unwanted affection can still show their real feeling.

A lot of you insist that your children kiss and hug family members and friends, even if they do not want to. Why would you teach, at such an early age, such a faulty premise; so as to be socially correct in other's eyes? and then wonder why in their later, grown up relationships they do not feel able to say no to unwanted things?

The "I am not your mate" thing, reminded Hannah of one time late at night waiting at a tube station for the last train home. A rather drunken, but happy and friendly chap was walking up to random lone ladies trying to give them a hug, with varying results, some of them surprisingly successful! Hannah had thought at the time; if he comes over to me wanting a hug like that, I might just punch him in the face!

After seeing my explosive anger as I raced as far from her as I could on those odd occasions she had 'matey-ed' me, my divine human had to look at herself and examine a thing she saw inside of herself that she did not like. I am glad to say, she decided that acting like we are all in it together having fun times when clearly all parties were not; was most definitely shitty behaviour that needed knocking on the head.

Can you see why, at times, we will look down our noses with derision at you, when you talk of us not having enough respect for you!

What other people think:

We do care about what you think, of course, because otherwise how does any being foster any relationship without acknowledging and knowing of each other's likes and dislikes.

But rather than dwelling on thoughts of whether we are liked or disliked, or approved of, or judged, like you lot do, we care much more about what is going on right now, in the moment. For instance; I step on your toe, you shout and leap in the air, I know you are unhappy about that occurrence. One minute later I am no longer focused on that event, you however are probably spending weeks afterwards telling all of this unfortunate incident, whilst two minutes after the event I could not care less about it, I am continually moving forward in the here and now.

In a secure well-adjusted being, caring about others comes from a base of understanding their own self-worth and having a good ability to express themselves, from having a feeling that they can be open without being judged, or not caring if judgement is passed on them, Hannah knew that I Washerpop, shed other's judgements of me as easily as duck sheds that water from his back. She wanted to be able to do that too.

Without having an inner peace and sense of security, a lot of you humans fall down, because, if you are still having that old paradigm going on where you look at others and compare yourselves to them and come up short, you will always have a lingering insecurity about you. If you must compare yourself, evaluate yourself instead, with who you used to be and revel in the knowing you now have, about things that you previously did not understand; celebrate how that now means you are able to change things in your life that you did not think possible before.

Comparing yourself to others or judging yourself by a societal ideal is a total killer of joy, every single time. Comparing your equines to other human's equines serves no good purpose either.

We seldom care that:

Other people's equines can do canter pirouettes and one time changes. And jump 1.20m.

How many ridiculous £££s the vet bill is.

How much any item at all costs, period. Money? What meaning does that have really? Well, you humans think a lot about it that is for sure! You may wish to think about how, if as you think it to be; if money is a finite resource to be divided up amongst yourselves and then fought over, how is it that there are many more millions and billions of pounds in the world now than there has ever been? That could not be the case if money didn't grow too, like everything else in the universe does.

Can you believe my ridiculous but lovely, but oh so ridiculous person did try to explain money to me once! The conversation came about because I am a breaker of many human things. She wanted me to; "please not break everything, thank you very much". Apparently, according to my human, things cost money and there was never enough money. I know there must be something amiss with that because nature is abundant and will always give us a way to thrive if we are open and can be believing enough to see that, and if humans do not shut us away from nature's resources.

Hannah recently came to us, quite cross about something; she told us a story of how some Donkeys she was looking after had stolen and eaten £60 from her coat pocket! She was cross because that money was meant to buy Henry Bear and I some hay to eat and she wanted us boys to join her in her indignation! Oh, this story did humour me, I thought I would quite like to meet these donkeys! They are obviously as intent on teaching my human what is important in life, as fondly as I am!

She had to go and tell some other humans all about it, as we would not agree with her that these donkeys had been spawned by Satan, specifically to persecute her.

Doing things in life just for the money, without love or fulfilment in what you are doing will always cause a feeling inside of you of lack, which then you dear humans try to fill with all the wrong things. Hannah learnt this because no matter how much money she earnt, she was still always chasing her tail. (I have not seen this human tail; she must keep it tucked in her pants) As soon as she decided to swap around how she thought and what she did and started to do things for the enjoyment and trusting that abundance would come somehow, then things started to dramatically improve for her.

Now, there are some things that we care about that you may not be aware of, and one of those is; what our equine peers think of us! Yes, we do have relationships within our species that do have similarities to some of your human to human relationships; we have others that we respect and listen to and others that we find disagreeable for various reasons.

We have herd leaders and a hierarchy of sorts, but this is dynamic and changing, it is not a 'one at the top' rule. One may lead us to safety, another may warn of danger coming, and these roles are interchangeable between individuals.

I wanted to be in charge of our little herd at one point, but the others were not interested in being led by a being that was going to take them all on a ten-mile panic gallop because a squirrel had poked his head around a tree. We have to be worthy of following.

But sometimes we can be led down a path by others too, much as you humans can listen to ill-conceived advice too, and only realise afterwards that it was not helpful to you.

Hannah wanted to teach me how to jump fences, she thought it would be fun, and it was great fun! Albeit short-lived, and I will tell you why.

Each day on going to and from my field, I would stop to converse with the big white horse in the paddock next door (if I made it that far). Hannah was always curious, as we would touch our noses, and then she could see some communication taking place between us. We would each nod, stop and pause and take turns, she could see us listening to each other, although of course there were no words she could hear to go with these actions. It reminded her of some occasions when human babies/toddlers, before they can form words, may be seen to be having a delightful conversation with each other or the family cat or dog, both engrossed in the conversation, with the grown-up humans not knowing a thing of what they are communicating to each other.

Anyhow, Hannah proceeded to introduce me to jumping, starting with wooden poles on the floor, in preparation for me then learning to jump over some raised poles, she did it all in the right way, slow as you like and starting without her sitting on my back.

The idea was that I would learn to walk, then trot, then canter calmly over these poles, and once I was calm and happy about that, we could progress to jumping over small raised poles and then doing the same things with Hannah riding me.

Sometimes I was indifferent to these poles, hardly noticing they were there, tripping over them. And other times Hannah thought it was as though she had set them on fire, I would make such a vast leap over every single one! And sometimes I would combine strategies and trip over one pole, jump over the next and then sharply swerve around the next one. I was not about to let those tricksy poles catch me out!

Hannah thought practice and familiarity were all that was required for me to come to know that all was needed was for me to step over these wooden sticks in a calm and comfortable manner. Each day I would converse with my big white horse friend as I went to the field, he told me some stories that fascinated me, about him and his human and the things that they got up to.

Each time Hannah took me for a session with the poles, I would improve with my calmness when they were on the ground. But as soon as Hannah raised one pole into a jump, (only a teenie weenie 6-inch increase) no matter how much practice I had at that, I would still jump as high as I could over the minuscule obstacle. I was clearly very keen and enjoying myself. No matter my human's communication to me that a 6-inch barrier only required me to make a 7-inch jump over it, I insisted on making leaps that would have cleared the big fence around the edge of arena!

After quite a few of these practice sessions, Hannah decided that she needed some help for when she attempted these things with me on board, we had done some walking and trotting over poles, with her sitting on my back, but she wanted some experienced guidance on the ground to try some actual jumps.

And so, a session was booked with our instructor. He rides event horses and is splendid at it so surely he would be able to help to sort us out.

We started our session off great, I was eager to show what I had learnt and quickly settled to walking, and trotting over the poles on the ground.

Now, Hannah knew that a strategy of this particular instructor was that he would casually say; "Just come around again" meaning; come and trot over the poles again as you have been doing. But he sneakily would have put a jump up without saying anything, so the unsuspecting rider would not have the chance to worry about it. But Hannah knew this instructor did this and looked around to see that he had made the last pole in the series into a small jump; only approx. 1 foot high. She expressed to this man that she was not ready to do that jump yet; he replied that all was going well and that Hannah could just expect me to trot over something that small as if it were no different to what we had already done.

Hannah knew different. She knew I would not necessarily do the logical thing and take this next step with a pinch of salt. And viewing this as a possible life or death situation for herself, she did not back down until this instructor had put one end of the pole back on the ground with one end raised by just 6 inches. "Are you confident to try that?" he asked her; "Oh...OK" she replied very half-heartedly.

I was more than glad to try that! I could show her I already knew how to jump and did not need these sessions with poles on the floor for goodness sake! Hannah asked me to trot, and so I popped myself up into a big forward bounding canter.

I knew I had to coil myself like a big spring to make the leap I had in mind, and we were off! I charged down the line of poles and at meeting the last half-raised one, I made the biggest jump I could, you should have seen it! I am just too fabulous!

The humans said afterwards I could have cleared the chicken shed outside the arena! I did some bronking after the fence, I was so excited and also not accustomed to the feeling of all of our combined weight going onto my front feet when we landed. I got told I was amazing and Hannah got told to try some more. Each try did not relax me into producing less effort and a smaller leap, I thought I would try to jump higher and higher each time! As it became apparent that I was not going to change what I was doing and Hannah had been very lucky not to part company with me so far, so we quit while we were ahead and still on a good note.

The humans were a little confused as to what to do, because my efforts did need commending, and they were very much praised, but at the same time, they wanted me to know that the idea was to do a small leap over a small hurdle, which we all could easily cope with!

We had a couple of more training sessions that went in the same sort of high jump/bronky fashion before Hannah decided we were good at the dressage and for the sake of her mental and physical health we would be doing dressage. Only. Dressage. For now. Until she recovered her poise on the subject of jumping. Once again, my human was horrified at how I just went off on my own tangent, regardless of what anyone else wanted or were guiding me towards and I seemingly didn't give a damn about how the humans want the game to be played because I was having the most amusing time playing the game my way!

A month or two later, an animal communication specialist was booked to visit the stable yard. Hannah knew this person, he had been before and communicated with Henry so she thought it would be fun, now that we had been together for about a year, to find out how I Washeroodle-doo, felt about my life now.

For those of you that don't know, this kind of animal communicator has become quiet enough in their own thoughts and feelings to be able to receive ours. Your human word for it would be "telepathy", or you would say that they are "psychic" but this to us is just a sense all of us beasts use as well as our other senses, we have not become reliant on words instead, as you humans have.

We use it amongst our species and to converse with other species too, and when we meet one such as this communicator, we are usually very pleased to be meeting with a human who can understand us in this way, who can perceive us more fully and let our carers know what is going on with us.

In this communicator's previous conversation with Henry; Henry had, had a vast amount to say. Lots of interesting things had occurred in his (at that time) 18 years of life in that big furry body, but one of the first things he conveyed through this man, blew Hannah's mind away;

Henry professed to be feeling somewhat embarrassed about his behaviour with big red vehicles when he was younger!

This message did not click for Hannah immediately, and then she remembered, it was so long ago, those times long forgotten!

Henry and I were living in the countryside at the time of this communication, but what the communicator did not know is that when Henry was 3, 4 and five years old, Hannah kept him in a very built up, busy part of West London. There were two rides you could do out of the front gate of the stable yard; if they turned left, it was a boring road ride. But if they turned right, there was a lane you could go down that led to some National Trust land and also some rough land that had not yet been built on. This ride was full of lovely canter tracks, and Henry would be allowed to take pit stops to eat some fabulous long green grass along the way. Henry very much preferred to turn right and go on that ride.

He had already proven, even by this early point in his life; not be bothered at all by even the largest and noisiest of all vehicles! Hannah was very confident to take him out riding anywhere, in fact, one day she found a show jumping show they could go to, so she rode Henry Bear up the very busy A4 main road and through Heathrow airport to get to this show! Aeroplanes coming into land 50 feet above the big Bears head and he did not bat an eyelid! (You are probably starting to see why I,

Washerpop was such a shock to my darling human)

Anyhow; one time Hannah and Henry were leaving the stable yard and Hannah's intention was to turn left and go around the boring road ride. There had been a lot of rain, and the fields would be very muddy and slippery to ride on. She waited for a gap in the traffic coming from the right, and gave Henry the signals to move on and turn left.

Henry wanted to turn right and have a fun ride. Henry is an immense, powerful horse, so he just ignored Hannah's left turn signals and turned right instead; straight in front of and oncoming bus! He was not afraid at all, he felt big and powerful and stood his ground, Hannah was very alarmed, as she did not see a face-off between horse and bus ending very well. But Henry calmly kept his course, and the poor bus driver managed to stop in time amid lots of apologies from Hannah.

Once Henry decided he had a choice, he thought there would be no more turning left ever again! After a few more similar incidences, Hannah got him a stronger bit, being young herself then and not knowing another way of staying in control of this bus teasing horse, and so left-hand turns were re-instated.

On another occasion around this time, Hannah and Henry had set out very early one Sunday morning to go to a park some distance away. Along the route, they came to a large road junction with traffic lights, they were planning to go straight on, and as they approached the lights, they turned red, and so horse and rider obeyed the traffic rule and stopped.

Hannah looked around and saw that a big red double decker bus was coming behind them and was indicating to turn right. She knew he was going to pull up right alongside them and stop in the turn right lane, and she also knew that when the bus stopped, its air brakes would release making a rather horrendous whooshing noise. Hannah shortened up her reins a bit just in case Henry got startled by the sound and propelled himself towards the moving traffic in front of them.

The bus pulled right alongside them and at the sound of the air brakes releasing, Henry pulled his ears right back in distaste for this large red vehicle, reached over with his teeth and proceeded to bite the big wing mirror right off of the side of the bus!

Hannah looked at the driver apologetically, silently mouthing a "Sorry!" The driver looked at her and kind of shrugged his shoulders. Then the right turn traffic light changed to green and he drove off. Henry, at the time, was very satisfied that he had taught that big ol' bus a lesson! Mr Bear hoped the other buses would hear of this and watch their behaviour in future, when the Mighty Bear was out and about.

But now, as an older more responsible animal, Henry Bear obviously felt he could have been a little less confrontational with these large red vehicles! Hannah had a warm glow in her heart, bless that Bear, for she knew, in 20 years of riding he did not need to be embarrassed or apologize for one single thing! She could never have been more proud of him, all this time.

So now it was my turn to have a visit with the communicator. As soon as this man entered my stable, Hannah knew I was going to have plenty to say. Instead of my usual fussing and grabbing at new people's clothing or shying away from them if I did not like their energy, Hannah was transfixed as I walked over to this man and stopped a foot away from him, I lowered my head and closed my eyes, no words spoken. I could feel him already, and I wanted to be heard.

The first thing he interpreted for me, to Hannah, was that for the first six months we were together I was not sure at all, having before had a pretty small view of all humans, but that now I love her and she loves me so much that I never want that to change.

That little glow in Hannah's belly grew into a great big fire; she knew this was true. She did also spend our first six months together thinking "what on earth have I done, fetching myself this horse!" only to find herself head over heels in love with me regardless of the many crazy things I did.

The next thing I was eager to let Hannah know was how very excited I was to be learning to jump! I relayed through this skilled interpreter, about how I was very excited because the white horse in the paddock next door to me had told me all about how to jump! Also he had told me stories of how he jumps and how he goes to competitions to show off his jumping and how everybody loves him for it! I told how this horse had told me exactly how to do it too! He had relayed to me how the humans just want you to jump as high as you can, the horse must not knock the jumps down, and the higher you leap, the more delighted the humans are!

Well, on hearing this from me through the communicator, Hannah could not keep the laughter down, it explained everything. Hannah knew this white horse well, he did indeed go to lots of competitions, and he did indeed jump very high, in fact, his humans did not believe much in training. They did not think that technique or calmness in the horse was needed; you point and fly at everything as fast as you can go, and you jump, high, high, high!

Much and more information was exchanged in this session, and afterwards as we walked back to the field, Hannah said to me; "You know Wash, it may be best if you don't believe everything that this white horse tells you, OK?" she felt like a crappy over protective mother who didn't want her precious baby knocking around with the 'wrong kind of kids', but she had visions of the time that this white horse had jumped out of his field and straight through a twenty foot high and four foot wide hedge! No one could find him for ages, panic ensued as no-one thought to look the other side of the impenetrable looking hedge, he was eventually found, munching on the neighbour's roses. So, no, Hannah did not want me getting any more good ideas from this one.

So, Hannah sent me images from her head, to mine, of how she would like our jumping to go, with small leaps over the small jumps, and I did listen; our next sessions were much more to her liking. She knew my over keenness had come from the same place that it does in you humans; of learning a new thing and wanting to be good at it straight away, wanting to run before you can walk, wanting to impress peers and diving straight in before any basic skills are learnt. It intrigued my human very much to learn that we can follow down these same paths as people do.

And she also learnt that we all do love to listen to a good story from another; the Dalai Lama is right; we do not need more successful people, we need love and fun and friendship and lovers and healers, and yes; horses like storytellers too, equine and human alike.

CHAPTER 6

BURDENS

"Being noticed can be a burden. Jesus got himself crucified because he got himself noticed. So I disappear a lot". ~ Bob Dylan.

You like to think that the equines in your lives, in western society at least, are no longer beasts of burden. They do not now need to carry heavy loads for you, or trek across miles of country for you, now that you have your cars and trucks, they no longer are your transport and are no longer deemed necessary to fight in your wars, on the whole.

But what is a burden? When someone tells you of a negative thing in their life, you will automatically make a judgement in your mind on that; A child with a terminal illness; That poor little thing you think, that young innocent life should not have to carry that burden. But what about the premier league footballer who earns £200,000 a week and goes off sick with stress? Get a grip, you maybe are thinking, for I would be happy to have that problem. And of course, there are all varieties of different situations between these two extremes.

But whether you think that football player has a point or not, he apparently is feeling burdened, even if his particular burden is not something you feel capable of understanding or being sympathetic of, from your very different perspective of life.

Maybe that £200,000 a week does not make up for his wife cheating on him, his brother dying of cancer and one of his favourite socks getting lost in the dryer, (the ones with little dinosaurs on) or maybe, he just is a bit of a dick. My point is though, that you don't know. You can never know what another being is truly feeling inside which means, if you wish to be a compassionate being, you must always give the benefit of the doubt.

Otherwise you will always be guided by cynicism, needing to judge others as lacking integrity, because your cynicism makes you believe that it is acceptable to judge others as guilty before proven innocent, instead of innocent until proven guilty, this misanthropy is what makes humans think that collateral damage is acceptable. That innocents suffering is acceptable. All so the small chance you may get walked on, duped, or taken advantage of, does not happen.

A burden may sound light or trivial on the face of it but may weigh very heavily on an individual, be they human or beast. All too frequently it is talked about how a mare in season can be "stroppy" to ride, or that one hour of work a day is not too much to expect from a horse in return for his keep. This kind of judgement makes the assumption that any reason the horse may have for not being able to perform on any one given day probably comes from laziness or belligerence.

How would any of you females feel if, when you had your period, which came accompanied by a sore back and tummy and a delicate balance of temperance in place, how would you feel if someone got on your back, pulled your head in and dug you in the ribs with their heels, expecting you to work, while calling you stroppy? Hannah knows as a human that if someone did this to her, she would probably be in prison for murder by now, yet at almost all of the many stable yards she has visited, it is common place to call a mare in season a 'stroppy bitch', and most of this name calling coming from female humans too.

If your horse is supposed to work for one hour a day, that might feel like too much to him if he has rolled on a stone and has a bruised back that you can't see. Or if he has gone in the arena the last four times in a row and wants to do something less stressful on his joints and something less mind-numbing, or if he has emotional upset going on around something.

A burden can be, just being around another being who views you as something you do not see yourself as. Do you like to spend time with people who quite happily share with the world how they think you are too fat, lazy, crazy, stupid, belligerent, moody or over sensitive?

Do you like it if you go in a shop and get followed by security when you are not a shoplifting type of person? Humans often decide their horses are lacking in integrity, with the only proof for that assumption being that the animal does not willingly buy into their bullshit.

You know, in your human to human relationships, you are wanting someone to be with who will be kind to you, who will nurture you and understand when you are sick or have had a bad day. You want one who can sooth you, who can have enough emotional intelligence to not give a crap if you blow up or meltdown; for them to still love you anyway.

But I can tell you it is a rare human who can give us beasts these things, but almost all people expect these things from us, you want them to be given freely and willingly. You try to persuade us that handing over our hearts, souls and physical bodies to you ones who don't even know how to look after your own, is a good idea.

CHAPTER 7

RESPECT

I try to discover...
A little something to make me sweeter... ~ Erasure, A little respect
(1988)

Much is talked by humans about respect and about how some of us equines need to show more respect in a variety of different ways.

Hannah had a lot of respect for her trainer, and he was always very positive, supremely knowledgeable, and he helped us both tremendously, but one day after our training session, Hannah had dismounted, and I decided a nice chew on her whip would be good. I love to chew on things! Also, I had a master plan to seek out, and destroy all of these sticks, the only time I did appreciate the whip was when it got used to brush horse flies from my belly out on those long hot summer rides.

Our trainer observed my destruction of yet another object, and he watched Hannah not doing anything much to stop that, and he said; "he is not very respectful is he?" Hannah felt some disappointment inside; she knew I did just as I wanted to do, quite a bit. Hannah knew she did not put me straight on things so much as other humans did with their equines, and also she wanted this trainer to think well of us. But then she was a little confused, as she thought, was I (Washerpop) really being disrespectful if she had not asked me not to do the thing that I was doing? Not really.

I would only be being disrespectful if I had been asked to stop something and then had not obliged. Partly Hannah let me do stuff like this because she knew from the previous occasions I would be highly likely to carry on doing as I please anyway, if she took the whip away I would stretch my head and neck down, pretending to yawn and bite her in the backs of her knees.

And mostly she liked me to be showing my cheeky side, although if I were a very well behaved creature, I would be admired by others, and of course, I would be easier to do things with. We did end up with quite a few convoluted practices to deal with different things, such as when Hannah would get on my back she would have to give me my treat for standing still, then ask me to move off very quickly before I would have the chance to swallow my treat, then swing my head around grab hold of her foot with my teeth and try to pull her back out of the saddle by her leg.

So, this incidental remark about me from our trainer did get her thinking on; what is respect and what does that mean anyway?

Dictionary definition:

1: To admire someone or something deeply, as a result of their abilities, qualities or achievements.

2: To have due regard for (someone's feelings, wishes or rights)

People talk about trust and how trust should be earned, and they also say the same thing about respect, but you guys are not taking into consideration what "respect" means to us, i.e. the other party.

Mostly you are only aware of the respect that you want, yes, you could say respect needs to be earned, so we will run with that a little before I tell you why it is an utterly flawed assertion to think these things can be earnt, like with your money.

So, let's say that Hannah needed to look at how to get me to respect her more.

Two ways you humans know:

Demand, using more force if not listened to, this would teach me to respect the fact that if I do not "mind" your wishes, there will be a consequence for me. This approach would maybe teach me that you only want me to show you the parts of my personality that you appreciate; that thing called conditional love again.

Or could she try to be more of a person who her horse would look up to? Again, what would this involve? Conventional training would say; good leadership? Setting a good example? Maybe Hannah could show me that chewing whips was not acceptable by not chewing whips herself. Now, of course, that does sound ridiculous! (Hannah did not chomp on whips, she is a bit odd but not that strange)

Well, what Hannah did not recognise at this time is that I did respect her very much, I respected her for NOT shutting down my personality, she respected that my sanity and being allowed to express myself was maybe more important than a £5 whip.

She did not know how to express what she felt in words. But she knew that a creature such as myself, knowing no bounds; when seemingly out of the blue (to her) took himself into aerial acrobatics with her on board for the flight of her life, she knew that the absolute last thing she wanted me to feel is that I could not express/give her clues as to how I am feeling about what we are doing at any given moment. All she had to go on were the clues when I did give them. Is he is happy? Is he is feeling cheeky? Is he is a bit stressed? There were so many times that she did not have any clue as to where some bizarre course of action I had embarked upon originated from, that she certainly did not want me to feel more so that it was against her wishes for me to show my feelings. She did not want them to be shut in, unseen, to then boil over at the point they become uncontainable.

My search and destroy mission for all whips comes from the fact that using a whip for direction is a flawed premise. What if we ignore the direction? You would have to give up and say it didn't work or escalate the whip from a directional tool to a weapon for violence? Where does that line in the sand sit? Is there any trainer in the world, no matter how good or how experienced who can definitively say where that line in the sand is? Some would say, so long as anger does not get used with it, all use is OK. You can hit pretty hard without anger, you can insult without anger.

You can direct us with your thought just as well as you can with a stick, but some won't do that because they know it takes away the power of having the ultimate say; the last word.

You are using the same techniques on us; (the fact that you "use them on us" shows how that is not cool, to begin with.) The same techniques used on you to get you through your schooling, or your physical workouts; "there is no gain without pain" "you have to push yourself to achieve!" Hannah could not figure out for a long time, when she came to me with this mentality, why I would do the biggest yawns, right in her face! Then she would get on my back, and I would go as slow as I could. If she came to me without this needing to instil some work ethic into me, I would move beautifully and swiftly from the slightest of signals; we two would become one, poetry in motion.

Do you think perhaps your treadmills and your rowing machines at your human gymnasiums should have a person stood by each one with a whip, ready to direct you with it towards developing a good work ethic if you slow down or if you have a wobble when your muscles get tired and sore?

Or is that not needed for humans because they can make up their own minds about when they need to take a break mentally or physically? You sit your weight on our backs and then tell us that you get to decide when we are tired or capable of doing more. That should be our choice. And as I have already pointed out: the only reason you would not yield to us in the moment of us tensing, stiffening or slowing, and push us instead; is out of fear. Because you think that we must learn to strive like you, or we will be forever taking the piss or just be worthless in human eyes, with your never ending endeavouring to get to the top of the pile.

You all sometimes wonder how your equines seem to get physically broken so often. Well, I will give you your answer: If you insist on being the one to decide when another's muscles, bones and mind have done enough, even though you cannot personally feel whether that mind or those muscles are fine or not. And if you also chose to see resistance shown by your horse not as a sign that he is struggling and needs a break, but as a sign that you need to get on at him to try harder? Then well, it is rather simple to work out why your horses are getting physically broken, isn't it?

Have you ever noticed how if you are joyful in doing something, if you are actively engaged in the activity, whether it is swimming in a lake or running up a hill, if you are doing it because you want to do it, because you have chosen to do it and are having fun doing it, then it seems effortless to you? That is because the energy can flow through you with no resistance when you are following your bliss.

So what does respect mean to you? Is it a one way street and you don't even know it? I felt angry that the whip was even there. Not shy of it or scared of it, but cross that the humans would rather poke at me with that thing than meet me as an equal and ask intelligently, like we could not understand something more enlightened than that basic limiting concept to move away from pressure, you dumb yourselves down when you dumb us down. You are like sheep herders who want dance partners, so unrefined in your thinking, you have no idea that we already know how to dance because you are trying to direct us like you would some sheep.

The problem with some of you humans and respect is that you expect the other to act first, you are not proactive. You say I will respect that being when they show me respect. You do not realize that for anything you want to come to you, you have to be the propellant of it. You have to act with mindfulness first.

There is a man who trains weights, he gets huge and strong, he does this because he was getting bullied as a teenager, he was puny back then and got picked on and beaten up. He wants respect, so now he is big, with big muscles, now he knows he will be ok if anybody messes with him. Goal achieved you would think? Now he will be shown respect.

But no, that is not the case, everywhere this man goes he has trouble, everybody wants to have a fight with him, because everything about him is demanding respect of others as he is not secure enough inside of himself to not need to demand it. Because his whole being, aura, energy is sending out a signal; do not mess with me, I will win, and because this is coming from a fearful place, he is unknowingly sending out a metaphysical message, a challenge to those who would mess with someone, and so violence appears into his reality. He has changed his body, but he has not changed his fearful mind-set, he only changed how his outer self looks not what he projects from the inside so he gets trouble still, despite all of his good efforts.

If you have to demand respect from another, it is not the other that needs to change; it is you.

You would only demand respect from a fearful point of view that you are not going to get shown any, that is the only time you would need to try the impossible: to force respect. If you know you are deserving of respect, then you would not have this anxiety accompanied with the need to demand.

You emit energy; if you have calmness, peace, and love and respect for yourself, then that is what others will reflect back to you. Some people think some horse trainers are magical; that they just have this magic touch. They do not know magic, they know (either consciously or subconsciously) how their energy creates their world, how it creates the vibration that Is then projected to all around them, interacting with them. They know how to be within themselves to then only get back what they wish in energy from others, again, it is not wizardry, it is something anyone can learn. Do you know why we equines love these trainers and will do all that they ask? Because we recognise something rare in them; they have stillness and calmness and a knowing that all can be achieved, so they do not need to push and demand. We can understand the simplicity then of what they are asking, and we do not need to think about how to respond because we know there is not going to be a backlash if we do not get it right. We can relax, be ourselves and have fun in the learning.

So now my human knew I did not need to be more respectful, she just had to stop insulting me with her sheep herding tactics, if she wanted to dance.

CHAPTER 8

THE HORSE CAN ONLY SHOW YOU WHAT YOU ARE WILLING TO SEE

You can't depend on your eyes when your imagination is out of focus. ~

Mark Twain.

Hannah could not understand for the life of her, why, when each day she asks for me to raise a hoof for it to be cleaned out, why I would never want to give it. Sometimes I would give the foot begrudgingly and sometimes I wouldn't give it. Before she could finish the task, I would always snatch my hoof back. Unlike a lot of horses who don't like to have their feet handled, I am happier about my back feet to be dealt with than my fronts. Practice and praise and rewarding good behaviour never made any appreciable difference to my attitude towards this.

Because gentle handling did not make any difference, it made my human think, watch and look a bit harder.

She wondered how she would feel about it as a human. Hannah thought about how cross she was at her work place, when they introduced a rule that everybody had to wear steel toe cap boots, even people who worked in the office and not in the warehouse handling heavy goods or operating machinery, had to wear them.

Hannah realised she was very precious about her own feet, she hated the feeling of pressure on her toes from the unyielding metal and the restriction in foot movement and she could take these shoes off at 5pm! She even bought boots a size too big and then she got blisters on her heels from her feet moving too much in the boot. She thought about how we must feel with any discomfort in our feet, especially shod, how we would have to accept a compromise to our physical wellness because of a human whim, our natural foot shape and balance altered and us having to adjust to that as a survival technique.

To be fair, Hannah's work boots were irritating more than painful, and everyone else wore them without a fuss mostly. But my human had always dreamed of going everywhere barefoot and never wore shoes when she could be free to feel her feet connected directly to the earth. What got her goat at work was the point that she was getting told what was best for her feet! They were her feet! How dare they tell her she had to compromise her own feet, how dare they tell her it was right that she should be uncomfortable every single day so that the day when a heavy thing may land on her foot and break a toe, should never come.

I Washerpop felt the same. It was as simple as that; they are my feet, it is my choice if and when they get touched. I, the same as Hannah, had felt pain there before and I wanted complete choice over what happens to my body, even if they were not hurting right now.

She thought how as a young child her mother had led her screaming out of hairdressers, doctor's surgeries and dentists after unsuccessful visits; Hannah had to laugh as she thought back and remembered these things for the first time in many years, she too had not wanted anyone to touch her without her permission!

Hannah thought of all of the times she had admonished me for biting and then she thought about the teacher she bit when said teacher had grabbed her arm to lead her forcibly, an unwilling participant, into the classroom. The nurse she bit when they tried to stick a needle in her arm and the extensive list of dentists she got banned from. It turns out no one likes to get bitten, no one at all!

Hannah thought about how those early experiences had shaped her adult views; it was still virtually impossible to get her into a hairdressers or dentist's chair unless the situation got desperate.

So what was Hannah's answer for me? Leave my feet until they are causing me a serious health problem and then drug me for treatment? Or find out how to change my perspective on being handled? Just being kind and patient had not been enough to do that.

Although now understanding of the thoughts that were leading to my uncooperative actions, Hannah did not know how to help me to change that. Not until she saw a video clip by a trainer, and it showed this lady handling her youngster's legs, she was kneeling and petting the horse's legs, spending some time not asking for an action, but just enjoying and admiring the beautiful things about the horse's legs, loving those legs! This lady waited until the horse wanted to give a leg, and then she thanked the leg! Hannah thought about how she would come to me on a mission, wanting my leg, being patient and calm to a point but then becoming demanding if I would not play ball, insisting because she saw it as her duty to take care of me physically, so she thought it perfectly acceptable to bulldoze through my feeling in the name of being altruistic.

Just like that teacher whose job it was to have children attend her class and for her to teach them, thought it was acceptable to drag Hannah kicking and screaming into the classroom, as it is being done for the good of the individual who's feelings and rights are being over-ridden. It suddenly clicked into place for Hannah what I had been telling her again and again with my actions! Goodness, she could not believe, once again how devoted I was to integrity and my teachings of her and that I would never give up until she could see where the change needed to come.

We both did a little happy dance.

The penny had dropped. Hannah had not only been coming to me with her shoddy altruism, she had also inadvertently continued on with what others had had started before her which perpetuated the cycle. She had been looking at my front legs. She had seen, again and again, the way my front feet turn inwards, how I had quite uneven symmetry through my shoulders from the way I carried myself. Seeing a fault there and looking at my legs as being faulty and needing fixing. She had been looking every day at my feet with negative thoughts and wondering why I gave her negativity back in this department.

Hannah had not liked it one bit when doctors, dentists, hairdressers and teachers had deemed her needing fixing. A hair style like she had been raised by wolves suited her just fine, why should she be forced to change it because it did not suit others? She had at that young age not grown so far away from knowing her perfection and not wanting others to look at her as faulty.

Of course, I did not want Hannah coming to me, as the hairdresser came to her! Hannah started doing some of the work with me that she had learnt. She told my legs they were good legs, they were beautiful legs, she just sat on the floor and stroked them, I liked this very much, it soothed me. I had carried this body dysmorphia, fuelled by human perception of me, from before I knew Hannah, she felt mortified once she realised what she had continued for me, but exhilarated to have found a way to help.

If you want something to change you have to be able to see the different thing you want and not just focus on the reality which you do not want. We can only show you what you are willing to see.

It did not take long, not long at all, Hannah would soothe my legs and feet with her thoughts and words, she would just appreciate them, and then she could see when I was beginning to be open to allowing. She would mentally ask if I could give a foot. If I was not ready, that had to be ok with Hannah! The first few times she got disappointed that I did not want to give to her. She stopped, she thought about how she could perceive others negative feeling towards her those times as a child, the disapproval, the disappointment, the frustration, she thought how that had made her want to run from them, not acquiesce to them.

Hannah practised letting me know that it was ok with her if I said no. Sounds liked a simple thing, doesn't it? but a lot of you humans are unable to do that.

Only once I was completely satisfied that me having an opinion different to Hannah was ok with her, did that leave a space, it left a space for me to think if I wanted to say yes or no! Instead of her having a negative vibration that made me automatically say no. Can you understand that? A space! While I was having disappointment and bad legs projected onto me, there was no space for a yes, I could only give a negative back to a negative. For the first time in over two years of Hannah trying to handle my feet, this time when she asked for a foot, I thought, do I want to give this human my foot? Hannah watched my face; she watched the expression in my eyes change, I thought, YES! I do! I surprised myself too! it was a new feeling to me, one of wanting to give as opposed to defending myself from the irritating and debilitating human thoughts.

I lifted and gave my foot to Hannah just from her thought, she was delighted and so was I. you may believe that this is a trivial thing. Some of you may think, what an incompetent human for sure, not able to gain an animals trust for foot handling, but trust me, anyone "capable or competent" coming with a "do as you are told" attitude would have got a very big lesson from me.

This change was an enormous shift for both of us, this is how easy things can be, some of you will have known that feeling when you have wanted to change something for such a long time, but just keep going around in circles no matter what you try. It is exhausting for you ones and for us to be offered the same negative feelings from you, time and time again.

Hannah could have argued all day long (and did for a long time) that I did have physical problems with my front feet, with my posture, the way I carried myself. Sometimes I was in pain because of these things and she as the human being in this relationship should do her utmost to fix these things. I bet there is not one of you out there who would disagree with that.

But can you see? Can you see that the very fact that Hannah came to me every new day and viewed my front legs as faulty meant that they could not be anything but that? She was keeping that reality alive for me.

My sweet human was very keen to understand this ideology more fully; she started to read and learn about a few more things. She looked back on other things that had happened and reaffirmed for herself that the answer to something is never in the same vibration as the problem, dwelling in, residing within the problem does not give you the answer.

So, she tried an experiment; she tried her very best, just to not look at my flaws. Only to look at me and think of me as the bright shining light that she did also see, not to discuss my so-called flaws with others, giving them a bigger part to play; making them a part of other people's realities also. Doing this did not mean she did not pay attention to any treatment I did need, but she gave as little air time to it as possible and all as positively as she could.

And she began to see the changes; I was so much more relaxed around her, not having to energetically defend or block myself against her ridiculous notions that I was less than perfect and "needed" her interference. As I began to relax, my physical stature began to change also, with no additional effort on Hannah's part; she did not get me the massage lady, the chiropractor, she did not focus on doing exercises to straighten me and supple me. She couldn't anyway; I would not stand for it at this time, she only got to this point of changing how she felt because I would not allow those things, I had bitten the massage lady and the back person, I had snorted with derision and set myself free from anyone looking to fix me that way because I knew that was not the way to effect change, my hooman needed to make a shift within herself.

And here, she did have another massive recognition about how humans must interfere almost all of the time, and where does it get you all? It gets you all tied up in knots! My human suddenly had an awareness of how arrogant it is of her and her species to think the only way things in the world can be better is if humans interfere with them, when in fact the reason most things are no longer whole and are deemed to need fixing is because humans messed with them to begin with.

Hannah recalled a time back at the beginning of the summer, the field she had acquired for us to live in had some fantastic orchids growing there, Hannah and the man who owned the field were delighted, five different species, one relatively rare. The landlord wanted Hannah to fence the areas where these beautiful flowers were growing so that Henry Bear and I would not accidently trample these gifts from nature.

Hannah knew that fencing off these little individual flower patches would very likely inspire Henry and I to become very interested in getting into the places we have been told we are not to go. She knew this from experience; Henry would reverse into the plastic electric fence posts and break them in half. I would get the tops of the posts in my teeth pull them out of the ground, sometimes I would go along behind Hannah and pull them up as she put them in, that was such priceless entertainment to see the look on her face when she turned around to see all of her work undone!

She wanted to tell this man, that nature does not need us to micromanage it, nature has its own knowing, its own order, and is perfectly well equipped to look after itself. But this lovely man was one of the few humans left at that time who did not think Hannah to be completely off her rocker, so she kept quiet. But she did not fence off these orchids either.

Each day she would walk around the field and check on them, they stayed in flower for six weeks or more some of them. Some of them were very close to the little paths we and the other animals (foxes, badgers and rabbits) had made for ourselves as the grass grew longer and longer, often it was quite hard for Hannah to spot these flowers, in particularly the small bee orchids.

I love to careen around the field every day; if it has been raining, I get a vast amount of energy with all of those fresh new ions zipping around in the air. I leap, I buck, I gallop, I spin and I pay no mind to where I am putting my feet. Hannah would see each day that the ground all around these little flower patches had been half trampled to death. But not one single orchid got stepped on by us, not until they had finished flowering. Now, Hannah knew that Henry and I had not been going around the field with a little mental note in our heads "must not trample the Orchids!" She also knew that it was not luck that they all survived unscathed, so that left only one other truth when you have already discovered that no occurrence in this universe is a coincidence.

It was simply a phenomenal example of us and the other animals and nature working in perfect harmony. It is not a conscious effort; it is a free flowing of our oneness that you have far, far separated yourselves from. We can do that when you humans do not get yourselves involved.

It is something we can all do together perfectly well if you humans do not think you know best and decide you need to interfere to make things better, to make them more perfect. Look around you, do you not all see the ultimate beauty, the wholeness that nature is? You can see it just in one leaf! You didn't come here to be policemen; regulating our grass intake for optimal wellness, governing our interactions with other equines so that not one has the risk of injury, you only have to do those things if you have already unwittingly taken away natures ability to show its perfection. Doing that by putting us on little patches of grass that do not allow us to metabolize properly through a natural amount of active movement over varied terrain, and a variety of different plant life to eat.

Sometimes you are raising us without a stable diverse group of our own species where we can learn how to interact without injury. I know that right now you all do not all have access to endless resources and acreage to change the environment in which your equines live, to one in which nature can do your work for you, but please do know that it is not your job to take away the balance that exists naturally and then chase your tail trying to replace it with some human concept which will never truly suffice and often brings you more problems.

Hannah's Mum said it perfectly, she was diagnosed with two serious illnesses, and she stated that she did not want to live her life like she sees so many others doing; getting given a medicine for one thing, that has side effects that make you sick in other ways, so the doctors give you medicine for that, which has side effects, that make you sick, so you get given another medicine for that, and on and on it goes. Before you know it you are rattling around with all of these pills inside of you, your entire life being about your sickness, and then you wonder why you cannot even begin to get well from there. Then your physical bodies cannot cope with so many chemicals and your internal organs can no longer function. Do you honestly think this is how you were born to live?

We are all born to thrive beyond what humans think is normal. Nature is perfect as it is; just so. Wellness can flow to all if that is the belief and that is what is allowed to happen.

Your scientists are discovering more and more about your body cells can completely renew themselves in days, weeks and months, so ask yourself if your body can renew itself that quickly, then how do you stay sick for so long? Because you have no trust or understanding in natures abilities to align for you and with you, you are far removed from your natural state of being, and so, rely on man management/interference. Not working out too well for you humans, is it? Sickness in your species is now endemic, but it does not need to be that way if you can find your connection again with nature.

CHAPTER 9

DISCONNECTION AND CONNECTION

'The Opposite Of Addiction Is Not Sobriety. The Opposite Of Addiction Is Connection.' ~ Johann Hari

I am a lover by nature, most of us equines are, but I in particular, am a very flamboyant expressive lover, not just a lover of female horses, but a lover of all.

I had not had much experience when growing up, of interacting with other equines or humans in a way that was meaningful or understandable to me, so as I try to show and express my love for others, I become labelled: riggy/coltish, aggressive and other such things.

My only intent is to love and to play, but because I get super excited about these interactions, I can be met by humans and horses alike with fear and disconnect. It surprised Hannah that it was not only humans who would disconnect from me in fear. She had assumed that the other horses would kick me if I got too annoying and then I would learn to respect their social norms and adapt my behaviour, thus be accepted.

But that never actually happened, no matter how many times another tells me to "get away" I do not modify my behaviour to fit in. And this is because social rejection causes aggression; this is why your human school shootings happen in America. I was in a vicious circle, but Hannah did not want to give in and subscribe me to a life of living without interaction with my own species.

I did not learn from my mother or other horses how to socially interact; I do not know how to approach another in a way they understand or how to groom or to be able to accept grooming. I am not sure how to ask or suggest; I only know how to demand and then become enraged at rejection.

Beings become fearful of what they do not know or understand (my not fitting into the standard/acceptable range behaviour in this case), and so they disconnect from it and disengage themselves from interaction as a form of defence.

Disconnection causes addictions of all kinds, I am a horse, so I do not have access to heroin or alcohol, but like humans who find other coping mechanisms, habits and OCDs, I have mine also, these addictions are my attempt to fill a void that the disconnection with others brings about.

I would come to others with joy in my heart and fair enough, maybe I will concede to an over-enthusiasm, brought on by my lack of interaction in the past and having had this intense wanting for a long time. But I come to others, and I say let us play, let us love, and almost to a tee, I am met with disconnect "we don't want to know you" "we don't understand you, so we shall shun you away in some form or other." The other horses did kick me, in my jumping for joy, the humans did wave their arms and chastise me, or were just plain fearful.

Hannah did try to explain to me about personal space and that I must try to allow others to approach me on their terms and that I need to heed their signals, for friendship to be able to develop. I thought they all had big old sticks stuck up their arses and I would get very cross about their rebuffs and the more they shirked away from me, the more desperate I became for some interaction, and so the more I would insist on it.

But I too did not want this cycle to continue, the disappointment for me was a big gaping thing.

So I did begin to listen and start making a little progress under Hannah's guidance. But as you humans do not like it if things are not instantaneously fixed, the other horse owners soon began taking their charges out of range of me; due to me being unable to change the only habits I had ever known, overnight, I did not get an opportunity to replace those habits with something better.

Hannah, although far from delighted with how these things were playing out for me, did have tremendous compassion in her heart for her blessed Washerpop. She knew! She knew how it felt to try to make friends or to try to engage a lover, only to have them see her enthusiasm, her big love and openness as not genuine or odd; something other than what it was, when it was just a simple thing of seeing something she very much liked, seeing a spectacular part of that person's inner being and unabashedly and innocently showing them you like that.

Hannah like me lacked in some social skills due to lack of interaction too; she had not fully learned that mostly other humans expected love not to be shown openly. (be it sisterly, brotherly or lover-ly love) She did not know that this would lead to ridicule and disconnect, she could not understand how when you love someone you cannot tell it to them in case they want to run away, she did not understand these rules. But she also knew that because of her lack of social play she had not got corrupted in her feelings like other humans, she had not learnt to shut her feelings down. She did know how to love very deeply and openly and no matter how some other people reacted negatively, and she knew this to be a gift she would be forever grateful not to have had schooled out of her at a young age by social conditioning and an urge to fit in.

My human saw I was the same in this respect, preferring to go it alone rather than fit in with what others expected of me.

Hannah had thought it was only the human world that seemed not to be able to take beings at face value and needed them to fit a particular set of criteria before you would be "allowed" into their lives. But it seemed these rules were there in the equine world too; there was only one horse that was prepared to spend time with me. He enjoyed my sense of humour and our silly rough and tumble games, but his people did not think our playing was appropriate, so he was taken away from me too.

The other people said I was bullying this horse, Hannah did try to tell them she thought we were just playing (hard at it, to be sure) and that all was well, she could see where this was going, and she did very much want me to have at least one friend.

When they first became fearful and took this horse away from me, they put my play mate into the field next door. Hannah got accused of letting him back in with me each day to play! It was not until one morning when they put this horse in the field next door and saw him jump straight over the fence and back in with me to play, that they saw the situation for what it was. They could not have been right about me bullying him if he enjoyed our play so much as to jump into my paddock for some more fun! Humans often prefer to be right, rather than to happy, so they took him to live at another stable yard.

With all of the other horses gone by now too, this left just me and Henry Bear and he still to this day will not play with me for even one minute!

Hannah got thinking about the other horses, were they right to defend themselves against me being rough in my over enthusiasm? Yes of course they were; she did do the same thing! She did not like me sneaking up behind her and trying to jump on her back either!

Were they right to not give me more chances because I quite often could not contain myself and blew my second and third chances?

She did all she could to help me and brother Bear connect a little more, we both enjoy the times when she puts herself neutrally in between us both and offers up treats or scratches and cuddles. These are the only times that we would relax into each other's company a little, we touch noses in greeting, as if we have never met before, let alone live 24/7 together! This would make Hannah smile, but she knew as a human she could not replace the socialisation I missed out on as a babe with other equines. She pleaded with Bear for a while to give me more chances, but she understood each time I leapt in the air and bit the top of his tail, why he would not.

Having seen how heartbroken I was every time interaction with another horse ended up in me being shunned, kicked or bitten (I would come tearing back to Hannah and stand with her, shaking, as she was often stood watching in the gateway), I would be utterly distraught that it had happened again. On a few occasions she would turn me out, and I would go galloping and squealing off towards the other horses, and then I would remember how it turned out before, and I would turn around come back to Hannah and ask to be taken back inside.

Hannah realised that the disconnect with my own species broke my heart, it broke hers too. She did not want me to have that from her each time as well, each time I ducked behind her while being led and had a nibble on the back of her neck. Each time I came to her in the field, so pleased to see her, and then snaked my head, threw my ears back and lunged at her.

But then she realised, the very second she thought my behaviour was going to turn into something overwhelming for her, Hannah would disconnect from me, she got ready for having to do something defence related, and I would feel that shift in her, and I would attack the disconnect.

Hannah wanted me to have some fun, not for me to be always disappointed, she was sick half to death of feeling she had to put up this defence mechanism too, and as I have said, she had got this far without any (much/severe) damage from me.

The next time I came charging up to Hannah in the field, ears pinned back, rearing and boxing, Hannah laughed and said "Wow Washeroo! Look at you! Look at your amazing moves! Let us play!"

So we played, we leapt and ran, and my human grabbed at the back of my knees like I did to her! Hannah did not know, to begin with, what to do without the line drawn in the sand; when she felt I was getting dangerous and she may end up missing a nose. So she just tried a few different things that were not defensive;

Star jumps

Walking like an Egyptian

Moonwalking

The crazy octopus arm wave

The important thing about these movements was Hannah's energy behind them without defensiveness, without fear that she would get hurt, she was able just to use moves to keep her space. And you could have knocked her down with a feather when I got a bit close, or she saw some real seriousness in my expression (shark, and in for the kill came to mind) that all she had to do was some flamboyant dance with lots of arm movement! Thinking of her space and just having fun in her space, and she could not believe it! I would stop what I was doing (leaping a bit too close to her head, or getting very close to getting a viper strike in rather than play acting it) and I would wait, with MY EARS FORWARD! Saying: mm ok, you are doing your thing in your space, I will respect that!

In this way, we could be together in a scenario that had previously caused Hannah to disconnect from me and that caused me distress which would have me shut out my love and show aggression. Now if I got too demanding and aggressive she could diffuse that negative energy, and we could be together in that space without that horribly disconnected feeling that made me lash out.

Disengaging with our loved ones is damaging for us both. Understanding why it comes will help; we all of us, equine, human or any other, disengage from that which we do not understand. That is why you can turn people and horses off from doing new things by over facing them, if your brain cannot process unwanted feelings and you are under pressure to push through them, a sense of dread will come next time you try. The disconnect comes from fear, and fear comes from a lack of understanding. You may think you understand what some situation is, but if fearful feelings come about it, you are not understanding the situation as it truly is.

Hannah did not have to worry that she had an aggressive horse that she needed to guard herself against and warn others of, even though that is what it looked like, for all the world to see. Hannah had a horse who was super excited about life, so passionately wanting others to play with, not knowing where or how to start, because he never had.

I did not need a muzzle, the whip, controlling, chastising or even just guiding to learn the error of my ways. I did not need to be told of my inappropriateness and to be disapproved of; I needed unconditional love, a big old hug and a playmate.

Addiction and compulsive behaviours:

Another thing that benefited Hannah personally as well as setting me free from her screwed up human perceptions is that we were both similar in that we both had compulsive behaviours. She could see in each of us, the way in which humans and horses can hold onto some habitual things that don't serve us, and by that, I mean holding onto thoughts and habits that are not conducive to having peace of mind. I was addicted to various habits; one was to be obsessed with touching the electric fence when it was on. I did not show any interest in it at all if there was no current going through it.

I am not shitting you; I enjoyed the thrill, the excuse to go nuts. Hannah would watch in bewilderment as I worked myself up to touching it with my nose. I just had to touch it, knowing full well what would happen! Often Hannah would not put the electricity on, and tell the others horse owners that she had forgotten or that the battery was dead, just so that I would not play with the power.

Compulsions and Addictions are mostly viewed by humanity in completely the wrong way. We all know that ex-drinkers and smokers are the worse people, is it just because they make you feel bad for not being able to give up something that they can? No, actually I don't think that is all there is to it, all you hear from these people is how they take one day at a time.

How they have to avoid situations with other smokers, drinkers or drug addicts to stay clean, how even years after not smoking, the smell of a cigarette makes them want one. After years of being sober, the ex-alcoholic still is not confident that they will be able to get through the next 24hrs without wanting a drink, dependant on what situations are served up to them and how stressful they might find those.

Hannah was interested in the correlation between my compulsive behaviours and hers. She knew that she either wanted to be happy to continue living life the way she was, imperfectly, but so what; or she wanted to be rid of her compulsions with ease. She did not want to spend the rest of life struggling when a stressful situation came up; wishing for a cigarette or a drink to help her through. And it did surprise my human that it is no different from her equine friends in how we develop habits to cope with stress. Not such a common sight anymore, but horses who crib bite or wind suck and just have some device installed on their stable to make it a practical impossibility for them to carry on with that behaviour, still show all the signs of stress, they just have no outlet for it.

Hannah knew that after all of the things we had accomplished together, that the only way she was going to be able to help me let go of my stresses was to be able to let go of hers and lead the march. She needed to come to me showing that she knew the world to be a fabulous place, not a place where we are constantly having to battle our own and other people's emotions.

She knew this was an occasion where faking it would not do, she would need to find real inner peace, to be able to show it to me.

She smiled wistfully to herself at that thought, had I Washerpop just given her an excuse, a reason, to let go of unhappiness, and selfishly dive head first into the undiscovered ocean of her true desires?

Hannah thought of her father dying when she was younger, she thought of how the worse thing about that was seeing him suffer, yes, but the other worse thing was the feeling she had lived with since, what that experience had essentially said to her, and made her believe, was that; life is shit and then you die. She realized, looking back on all of that, so many years later, and now with a Washerpop all of her very own, to make her think more, she saw how her feeling that the world was hopeless had shaped her views on a lot of things, views that no longer held true for her.

How could they be true now? for some divine, unseen entity had sent her a Washerpop. What a clever universe. What a clever horse.

If there is one thing you want to be showing your children, only one rule to have, have this one: Try your best to show them, through letting go of your insecurities, anxieties, grudges, worries and woes, as easily and as quickly as is possible for you, show them that you do indeed believe the world to be a marvellous place, a place where it is possible to thrive. Then they will grow and flourish no matter what gets thrown at them. Without that, with a feeling that the chips are always stacked against them, any being will always be looking to fill that void, or drown the feeling out with compulsive behaviour and addictions of some kind.

CHAPTER 10

OUR MISBEHAVIOURS

"He has no choice. I'll have no man telling me to shave my fuckin' legs. Shave yours."

Adele ~ on being asked by a journalist what her boyfriend thought about her not shaving her legs. (2016)

If I knew who this Adele person was, I would give her a big Washer kiss (and not the Glasgow type kiss I have been known to give either) I like her, I have said the same kind of things to Hannah;

As I grabbed the lunge whip and chased her "Why don't you go around in little circles until YOU get dizzy!"

As I pushed that lovely but misguided instructor into the ditch; "YOU go in the ditch if you think it is so good in the ditch!"

You do not like what you see as these "misbehaviours", but as we do not speak your words, this is how we show you what we are feeling.

How about you humans make a change from calling us names:

Naughty

Bad

Belligerent

Lazy

Silly

Stupid

You will hear some form of this type of language on most stable yards every day.

How about some of you hoomans be honest with yourselves and change those belittling words to;

"My horse is not naughty, bad, belligerent, lazy, silly or stupid; I just refuse to take responsibility for bringing this animal into my life and not recognising the fact that he did not ask to be born into captivity. He did not ask for me to sit on his back and he is intelligent enough to know his own likes and dislikes and has every right to choose not to participate; so I call him naughty, wrong and uneducated. Because I speak words and he does not, I judge him as a being of lesser intelligence and in that, I assume a right to bulldoze over any sign he may give me that I am not half so clever as I think and that I in fact lack in a basic compassion and humility that my beast has in bucket loads, or how else would he allow me to be sitting on his back. If I am totally honest, I expect my horse to be like a motorbike, to perform in perfection as described in his "for sale" advertisement and to be happily disregarded at all times except when I want to ride or want comfort or want to grace him with my presence for whatever reason."

How do you like them apples?

Why do so many humans wish to talk of their little ones and animals as being troublesome for not agreeing with them on every single point that there can be? Why do you equate getting another being to go along with what you think is best, with success? Surely the success lies in understanding each other and then finding ways of doing things, and finding things to do, or ways to do things that satisfy both parties?

Do you not know how much you limit yourselves and us by thinking the whole point in life is to get other beings to agree with you? You shut out the magic and the potential for anything new to come, by not being willing to meet us as equals and then go from there.

My human has seen that now, I have shown her that. I do not like to call her dense, because she, like you is not lacking in good active brain cells and does have a heart full of compassion. But her head was so full of so many different thoughts; many learnt from what others consider to be "right or wrong" that she could not hear herself, her feelings that need to be acknowledged and listened to, and she certainly could not hear me. She could not hear me until I gave her no other option. If you weigh 600kg and act like you are going to jump on the humans head enough times, then they can start to listen to you. Then maybe the human can accept that they need to shift their mindset: to try a different way or take up knitting.

You have many different names/reasons you give for our so-called misbehaviours; Opinionated, stroppy, lazy, and all the rest. What you need to see is that all of our behaviours, whether you deem them good or bad are telling you something. I don't know how many times I can say this or how many I will need to: "WE DO NOT USE WORDS" you know that. So why, when we tell you without words; "I am in pain" or "I am not understanding". Or "you are sitting on me in such a way as I can't move how you want me to". Or "I cannot give you my undivided attention while figuring out if this thing may be a threat to my safety" How is it, you can translate this into; "acting like a tit" or "being silly" or "naughty"!?

Humans could and would be better at teaching other people and us horses and our other animal friends if they could get over needing for the one way to be right, this method, that method. I taught my human the folly of this by listening each time she had a new idea, learnt from others or thought up by herself.

I would participate out of interest of what the new thing was, and then much to my human's confusion and disappointment, a few days later it would seem to her that I had completely lost enthusiasm and did not want to participate. It took a while, but now she knows, it is not what she does, or what we do together, but how we do it that matters.

If a thought from a human on a thing to do is coming from a place of fear, fear of what the horse may do if not kept in his place, if not taught his manners; a place of needing to control, instead of a place of love, then the human is starting off by grabbing the wrong end of the stick. The person will be trying to push the car up the hill with the handbrake on, so to speak.

Thoughts from a place of love start with things such as: "What can we do together today? What can I do differently if this horse would rather not engage with me on this subject?" (A note to all you knowledgeable ones here – you might want to drop the subject, if only temporarily)

Thoughts coming from a place of fear start with things like: "if I let him get away with that then he will walk all over me next time" and "I must be more assertive and dominant for this horse to listen to me."

If a new training method is being employed to gain a different response, but the human is still coming to the party with thoughts of "fixing" or "telling", nothing will change much. With only being able to see the problem that needs solving so strongly that they have no room inside themselves for a solution to form, then you can go as far as lobotomizing us or flying us to the moon and back, it won't make one lasting bit of difference. I will ask you all a question here; do you like it when anyone, a boss, a husband/wife/lover or friend views you as faulty? Views you as not enough as you are? No, I thought not. We don't like it either. Train us to do things, by all means, some individuals can and will enjoy participating in this stuff with humans. But look at where you are coming from before you start, try listening to us along the way, and you won't need to ask anyone else how to do things, very often. You will know what is right because we will be your guides if you are listening to us.

Humans take such effort, such anxiousness in their strivings to achieve, so much worry of all that can go wrong, we all of us want you to have more fun, all of us to a tee, more fun with what you do, by trying less, more can be achieved. I will show you here all the things I showed my human, and NOW she knows how to live; NOW she knows how to love.

Do you know that every thought or feeling that you project towards us, we can feel? An old saying of yours "horses can smell fear" is not quite right although you do emit odour. But we receive the emotion that you are feeling, you think you hide it sometimes, but you don't. It is the same thing as when your dog or cat "knows" you are coming home, we feel your intention, always! If this is new information to you, please don't be alarmed and fear to go near us all together in case you can't keep a rogue thought from coming. Instead, trust that we will always show you in whatever way we can that we have noticed how you feel and we want you to become aware of it too, and get yourself to a better place that is conducive to us all having fun together. There is beauty in this, and a real way forwards, an opening of a door that leads out onto a lush utopian grassland full of all of the things you desire.

CHAPTER 11

COMPASSION

'Love and compassion are necessities, not luxuries. Without them, humanity cannot survive.' ~ Dalai Lama

If you can get this one right then the rest of this book is just a bonus really; most people make this mistake of going through life as you have been trained, thinking that you love but having no real idea of what that truly means or how to achieve the loving relationships that you want without being a doormat. You have been socially conditioned to believe things work a certain way and then you try to fit your relationships into that tiny box, swinging between feeling unheard and then pushing hard or demanding to be heard, neither party feeling any real freedom or fulfilment. Hannah was this way too, so I showed her the part of life she could not see while looking through that small lens.

All beings are deeply compassionate and loving inside, but most of you can only love your family or be loving towards others when conditions are right, or when the ones you have relationships with are acting in a way to please you. On meeting new people you do not want to open your hearts straight away, you want to find out how they behave and what they think about things and then you judge whether they are worthy of your love or not before you will give it. This makes complete rational sense I am sure, but unwittingly you are continuing the separation that humans commonly place between themselves and others as a form of protection, whereas if you shift to going at it the other way around, meeting all with an open heart, every being then has the opportunity to respond to you with their best selves.

On meeting others, you want to know things such as where they live, what jobs they do and what achievements they have accomplished, then you can judge their worthiness of your attention, time and love.

Try this for one week; begin approaching others with openness and love in your heart, let go of as much judgement as you can and set your intention to discover what beauty is at the essence of the beings you interact with. You may be very surprised at the different tracks your conversations take and at how much more gratifying meeting others on these new terms feels to you. Aim for true connection; know that the things you may fear about having a real openness about yourself cannot come to you if you come with a vibration that allows others to show you the splendid things about them.

You are an infinite source of love, you are love, and it is not a finite resource to be dished out in little bits and pieces to those who you judge to warrant it. It is your natural state of being which you may have forgotten, but can easily remember once you start to practice it again.

And yes, of course, some beings are easier to love than others, with a friend, lover, child, horse or pet; you will behave lovingly towards them until some behaviour from them makes you think/believe that they are wrong and you are right. Then there needs to be conditions; so and so needs to do this or I will be forced to do that. This scenario causes a bad feeling always; never does any being feel good about getting on at our loved ones, never. And you are unconsciously conditioning others around you that to be accepted they must always behave in a way that pleases.

Can you feel how stifling that is? Then you wonder why your kids do drugs. Your lover runs off with another, and your dog chews the legs off of all of your chairs.

Here is the deal, here is what you gorgeous but misguided humans have been getting arse about face, and it is so important. The reason people cannot allow themselves to show compassion is because the common belief is that if you show compassion and kindness all of the time that at some point you will get walked all over and used and disrespected.

But, in fact, your strength needs to come from inside to allow you to be soft and open with others on the outside. If you have an un-moveable knowing and belief (yes this may take time to develop) inside of you, that you can choose your emotions, that no one can force you to be unhappy about a situation or a person, if you can know that is a choice you can consciously make, whether to judge or not, whether to mind at an opinion adverse to your own, or not, then you will build an inner strength.

You will develop a thing called emotional maturity, or emotional intelligence, and I am sorry, but most of you humans have little to none of it! Developing emotional intelligence is by far, way, way more important to you if you want to be living a happy life, than an academic degree on paper. You ALWAYS have the choice to respond differently to circumstance, and if you meet others with softness, and gentleness about you; they will start to give you the same back or they will not be able to interact with you on that level at all and will disappear from your life. You can only fight fire with fire; the same vibrations attract each other. Guardedness attracts guardedness; anxiety attracts anxiety and compassion attracts compassion.

You can see how we equines know this? You project your inside the box thinking onto us a LOT. With the view of love being a limited resource and with your being unconscious of like attracting like, you try to fight the things you don't want in your lives with more of the vibration/mood/feeling that caused the problem in the first place.

With this mindset, there will always come a time or a situation that will make you think you have to hold back your love and lay down the law, and this will always feel bad to you inside because your inner self is loving and caring.

The misguided belief that most humans have is that to be selfless, to give or be compassionate leaves you open to all sorts of unwanted. The opposite is actually true; you need to be selfish to be able to give, you need to care about your own feelings first and have that inner knowing and emotional robustness to be able to have anything worth giving to others. Sounds upside down yes? Hannah has discovered most of what I have taught her seemed topsy-turvy at first. She began by thinking me crazy and ended up knowing I could teach her everything.

A lot of what we horses are trying to teach you is about love. Do you know why you love us so much? Do you know why you feel the need to have us beasts in your lives, why it feels so good to have that cat sitting purring on your lap, why it feels so good to come home from work to that waggy dog tail? Why you love the moment you feel our gentle breath on your neck? Because we are always showing you, love is the way; the ONLY way. We are showing you that you worry too much, let it go, let it go, let it go! And do you know why you do not, or cannot? Because you struggle to think we are of equal intelligence to you, you think we have things to learn from you, but you do not think we have important, intelligent, worthwhile, lifechanging things to teach you.

You have got to admit it, most of your species think if the beasts are happy it is because they are too stupid to comprehend the things that humans are unhappy about! Common sense makes you want to believe that most of the entire human population cannot be wrong in their mass degradation of us beasts, look at your farm animals. There is no way you could or would treat them the way you do if you knew they have an equal or perhaps a higher consciousness than you. Maybe you think that we do not understand the trials and tribulations and responsibilities of what it means to be human, oh, how wrong could you be, oh, we so do know.... Why do you think we comfort you so, and try to show you how it could be different from that for you?

And still, our answer is the same, Love, love and more love, yes! You have bills to pay! Yes, your boss was horrid to you today, but you can't quit your job because then you wouldn't have money to feed us! Do you know how come we do understand that? Because we feel the frustration and despondency, or anger; a grievance emanating from you, we also experience these same emotions; every time we do not move forward because something somewhere is sore and you tell us we are opinionated and apply your will for us to go forward more strongly. Every time, we feel the same feelings of being ridden roughshod over, of not being understood by you, we feel the same frustrations and hurt that you do. And we know the answer is LOVE! That is why most of us will take quite a bit of crap from you before showing you anything other than love because we know the answer is not in rubbing up against what we do not want.

But a lot of the time you can't hear what we are saying because you cannot focus on showing love, being loving. Seeing a lack of compassion in everyday life and on your televisions, fosters a fearful 'life is not fair attitude' and a 'learned helplessness' about it. You say, well this is the way things are. If you perceive life is not fair for you all or life is tough, but you have to "suck it up" then you think we have to suck up mediocrity too, having our thoughts ignored, living a second-class life. And what all of us beings want in life is the freedom to expand and to express our expansion as we choose. So we do know very well how you feel about your human dramas and traumas. Very well.

Did you know, I don't mind a bit of being a riding horse, it pleases my human, and when she gets it right and I feel good for it, then we have some awesome fun times. But I see a life of being a riding horse as quite limiting for me; I like to expand in other ways. Did I tell you I am a poet?

I like to watch the autumn colours changing on the trees. I like to listen to the whispers on the wind, sometimes reassuring and sometimes haunting me, but I like to listen anyway. I love the crunch of the autumn leaves under my hooves; it evokes in me a real feeling of connection and joy that makes me kick my heels in the air and squeal and run in delight. I love to taste everything; I am curious about all human-made things, I cannot hold them in my hands, as I possess hooves in this life, the taste of different coverings you put on your wood, and the taste of metal things intrigue me.

I am an explorer at heart, and so are all of you, that is why you are happy as young children and not so much as adults, you stop exploring.

There have been a few humans come into my life who can actually hear us beasts, with these ones I have shared my poetry. I have told of how my emotions change with the changing skies and the changes in atmospheric pressure, of how my heart bleeds when I hear the screams of trees being cut, of how tired I was of being told to "man up" by the humans. I revealed how my essence is one of exploring mine own and others sensuality and sensitivity, I am no 'Bear Grylls' type, by nature, but that does not mean I am not robust. Do not ask a fish to climb a tree and then be disappointed when it cannot.

And of course, I did not share this deeper, wider part of myself with those who showed me the stick, or with those who tried to define me by their limited terms, those who cannot hear.

We are all different things, some of us teachers, some of us are your healers, some of us may define ourselves by our role in our herd and not at all with being a "riding" horse, you call this thing separation anxiety, because we do not deem being with our human as more important or more satisfying than being a part of our own family.

We want you to learn our language, and we want you to know who we really are, and to acknowledge these different parts of us. But this is difficult because most of you don't even give yourself time or permission to explore and discover who you may really be. To learn what delightful, diverse components your personality is made up of, because you rather narrowly steer your lives in a straight line of job, food, television and policing the kids, you know this is not entirely satisfying, but you do not allow yourselves an open path to much else.

You may be thinking by now, as Hannah did; Bloomin heck! This Washerpop wants us all to have perfect lives! He is a hard task master! And yes I am a hard task master, but I do not want you to have perfect lives, I want you to know there is so much more love, life and laughter available to you than you can see. If you start to open yourselves up to that idea, it will not be long before you awaken every day with a feeling of such wonder and love for the planet that you reside on and for all the beings sharing this place too. You will be thankful of the diversity; able to embrace difference instead of forging blindly ahead down the path of conformity. Passion, compassion and love will become the easiest and first thoughts and options to you. Yes, heaven really is a place on earth.

CHAPTER 12

I DON'T KNOW... WHAT DO YOU WANNA DO?

Buzzie: [to Flaps] Okay, so what we gonna do?

Flaps: I don't know, what you wanna do?

Buzzie: Look, Flaps, first I say, "What we gonna do?" Then you say, "I don't know, what you wanna do?" Then I say, "What we gonna do?" You say, "What you wanna do?" "What we gonna do?" "What you want..." Let's do SOMETHING!

Flaps: Okay. What you wanna do?

Buzzie: Oh, blimey! There you go again. The same notes again!

Ziggy: I've got it! This time, I've really got it!

Buzzie: Now you've got it. So what we gonna do?

The vultures; Jungle Book – Disney Productions (1967)

My human used to say to me all the time: "I don't know Washer". Sometimes she would tag on the end of that: "what are we going to do with you Washerpop?" When Hannah first started to be able to be a bit quieter within herself and then began to hear what I was transmitting to her clearly, the first thing she kept on hearing from me was "Oh, but you do! You do know! You DO know!" I relayed this same message to her so many times that she knew she did not imagine it, so she had to consider what I was meaning by it.

Hannah thought about the times she said "I don't know!" she said it to herself all of the time, arriving at work on a Monday morning, to a job she did not find fulfilling. She would silently ask herself what on earth she was doing there and then the answer would come out loud from her mouth accompanied by a big sigh: "I don't know!"

After quite some thought she realised that if she was honest with herself, she did know the answers, but was denying herself them. Continuing to go around saying "I don't know" because it exempted her from having to take any action, it exempted her from having to be brave enough to do something different.

Hannah did know the answer to that Monday morning feeling at work. And she did know the answer to the problems she had with me, but she said; "I don't know" because change scared the bejesus out of her.

She knew the answer with me was for her to listen more at a time when she was already the subject of criticism for treating me as little Prince Washerpop. The consideration she was already giving to my feelings, in other's eyes meant she was not "getting after" me enough, or "telling me" what to do enough.

Humans were wondering why I would not acquiesce to their needing to put me beneath them on a scale, intelligence and rights wise. Instead of 'human rights' and 'animal rights' there should be 'being's rights' they should be the same for all. I knew I had the choice with Hannah. What was maybe perceived by professional horse trainers as Hannah being a walk over and needing to assert herself onto me, was her knowing that she liked me standing up for what I wanted, even if it did embarrass her in front of others. How could she say no to me having what she also wanted for herself? To feel free of judgement and to participate in things with other beings on terms that are fair to all parties? Hannah was frightened because she felt she was not understood by people at the best of times and knew that going down a path away from the traditional horsemanship she had vaguely followed and that all around her swore by, would make her even more of an alien in the other human's eyes.

But my person kind of knew by now, there is no turning back, and she had another saying too; (much better than 'I don't know') She had started to say; "we haven't come this far, to only come this far" I liked this one, so we went with it. It meant breaking through some barriers.

Hannah stopped saying I don't know, and she admitted that she did know that I and other animals are sentient beings and that it may not be fair for her to insist on domesticating me and sitting on my back, no matter my thoughts on the matter; she was sick of cajoling all of the time. She did know that it wasn't fair for her to expect me to be happy with life conditions unsatisfactory to me, not dissimilar than the conditions that had previously turned her to cynicism and alcohol; being expected to go along with a life designed for you by others. She knew that the life conditions I was against weren't physical things that needed changing such as stable yards, amount of grazing and things like that, but the conditions imposed on me by the ingrained human misguided beliefs. The generally accepted life circumstances of having your feelings ignored or belittled until you get to the point of not daring to show them.

Who am I to dare to move against the crowd? I am all things, and everyone.

With this change in her mindset, Hannah noticed a difference in me immediately. Some of you knowledgeable ones and Hannah's instructors would have approved of the change in me; I appeared to have become more acquiescent. To outside eyes, you could have perhaps said it came about by Hannah being less wishy-washy and taking a leadership stance with me. But she became more confident and relaxed with me because she became more definite in her thought that dominating me and having me submit was not what she wanted.

This softening in her is what softened me, she became strong in her convictions on the inside which enabled her to be softer on the outside. I became more eager to follow the human's wishes because she simply gave up her viewpoint of accepting less for herself and then being exasperated when I appeared to want more. She saw that me wanting more was inspiring; this thought opened up doors of possibility. Hannah joined me by having more respect for who she is and who I am, not for others opinions on the subject.

Hannah joined me in following her bliss.

And then one day she said to me: "What do you wanna do Washerpop?" and for the first time in my life I said; "I don't knoooow...what do you wanna do?" and I followed her lead.

CHAPTER 13

FINDING YOUR POWER

Power does not corrupt. Fear corrupts. Perhaps the fear of a loss of power. ~John Steinbeck

Hannah could tell that I knew my own power, and this fascinated her. She knew because although I could resort to high aerial acrobatics or viciousness to get myself heard, I more often than not, chose just to hold my power. Hold my own space and not to allow myself to be rocked from that standing place by any others.

Hence a lot of my teachings involved me just doing nothing when asked to do something. The best leaders do not need to scream and shout to be heard, they are heard by the energy they exude.

People tend to think that power is something evil or something that should not be searched for or wanted. A lot of your films have the "bad" person wanting power, to rule over others unfairly, so you end up equating power as being, malignant, narcissistic, cocky and arrogant; in opposition to humility, and equality, but that is not right at all.

Every individual's power lays in being at peace inside of themselves and not needing to change others or outside circumstances to feel in harmony.

In fact, if you cannot realise your own power and feel happy and stress-free to hold your ground when something matters very much to you, or when another being or event challenges you; then you are giving away your power in a detrimental way. If you cannot stand solidly within your knowing and say to others; "I have heard what you say, but I am happily choosing to do the opposite because I was not put on this planet just to please you" If you cannot feel free to say that, then you will feel trapped and cramped and be wanting to find ways to get off of the hamster wheel you have created for yourself. You will feel hurt, begrudging and unheard, and you will need to go and tell others about how crap this person is or that situation is. Then you will just be hanging out with a bunch of individuals who believe life is rough, random, and not likely to change, all agreeing about these terrible things. You then have no access to anything different.

Take your power, stand in it as I do, do not give away your whole self in an attempt to bring happiness to others, it will never work for long, accept responsibility for yourself and your happiness because only you can choose how you feel in relationship to others and outside circumstance.

One time when we had not been doing our riding for very long, Hannah got on me out in the field, she gave me a pat on the neck and leant down to give me my treat for standing quietly for this bit. Then she gathered up her reins and put her legs against my sides, this being the cue for me to move forwards.

Up until now she had been wearing kid gloves around me, keeping her movements small and delicate so as not to panic me with any rapid movement or sound (I could panic very easily) and she would use her legs very gently, so as not to cause me to zoom off into orbit. On this occasion when Hannah put her legs against my sides and asked me to move off, I just shut my eyes and ignored her request.

So she asked more forcefully, and I ignored her some more. This led to increasingly ridiculous attempts from her, to get me to move my feet: she was waving arms, flapping reins on my neck, making noise, I can't be sure, but I think she may even have used the stick! I did not bat an eyelid I did not tense against her, or put my head up or my ears back, I thought about slipping in a yawn, but that may well have finished her off... even I know my limits.

Hannah's friend came out and tried to lead me forwards, and then tried to shoo me along from behind, to no avail. Hannah got off of me and tried to persuade me forwards from the ground; I remained: eyes shut, ears forward, feet planted; so she got back on.

Then my goofy human ended up sitting on me backwards! Me! Crazy, spooky Washerpop! I have been described by one instructor as being 100 times sharper than his sharpest horse. Hannah was now sitting on me back to front and slapping me on the bum with both hands, shouting "Move now please Washer!" After about 10 minutes of trying all different things, Hannah swung herself back the right way in the saddle (facing forwards that is) and flung her arms in the air. She let out a big sigh, looking up at the skies and said; "Ok Washer, you win, I give up!" as she sat up on my back, no stirrups, no reins, arms now folded, and I said; "ah...you give up! Well done human! Now we can start!" I opened my eyes, blew my nose and marched off up the track.

Any average competent horse person would say Hannah was being wet and needed to take me in hand, but she just knew, if she had gone down the route of escalating into violence, that I would have stood there pretending to be asleep while she beat me raw. She did not want that despite how useless she may look to the other horse owners, and she was fascinated by what had just occurred. I could have a leaf fall off a tree and land on my head and decide that going straight home at top speed was advisable, the world just being too unsafe. I got chased by my own shadow once, and once by a bee! I still do not trust the gutter that drips in the rain. And here, now, Hannah knew I also could, very precisely, on occasion, when I chose to; quite happily pretend to be asleep while my rider did everything she could to poke at me, trying to agitate Washer the wasp's nest into action, well that's a lesson, just right there.

Hannah was secretly delighted that I had no trouble in saying no! I did not like the attitude she had come with that day, it was only a small thing, but a critical thing! Things had been going well, and she had got to assuming that I had become a good little riding horse, acquiescent and subservient to her every whim. I wanted her to come to me fresh each day without these kinds of assumptions because I knew where that was leading.

Hannah had human partners in the past, and she knew from experience, that at the beginning of the relationship they would get on like a house on fire, but the minute they settled into the relationship and started expecting the other to behave in ways pleasing to them, that things would go downhill from there. Demands would get made, even if silently, and disapproval of non-compliance quietly hung in the background, bleeding the fun out of life.

She recalled a time when she had chosen to take Henry Bear on a fabulous cross country ride instead of attending big family Sunday dinner with her partner's relations. She had known the dinner would consist of tedious chit-chat and unwanted probing questions about her life, designed to seek out her worthiness or lack of it.

She remembered feeling resentful at being made to feel guilty for choosing to do something she enjoyed instead.

The reason my resistance to her desire to get me to move made her squeal with delight, in the end, was because she realised what it was I had shown her: no one else can make you feel bad for doing what you want to do. I certainly did not feel bad in standing my ground and saying; "I will come riding with you, but not if you think you can make me do it, or cajole, sweet talk me, or guilt me into it. Oh, and not if you are just going to expect it and take it for granted either."

She knew right then, that there is no point in doing what you want to do if you are going to allow others to make you feel as bad for pleasing yourself, as you would have by going along with what they wanted you to do. She knew now she would be able to stand in her power too, in all relationships and know that her happiness, like mine, did not need to depend on another's actions, reactions, or their approval.

What this and other examples I gave, also taught Hannah was that each of us as individuals can only know what we want. Someone else cannot know for us. She would often give her power away to others who she thought more knowledgeable or ones who could guilt her into behaving a certain way. I showed her that our real power lays in knowing how we feel and making decisions for ourselves. By all means, listen to others, but if that advice goes against what you are feeling is right inside you, then notice that and give it validity, you do not have to do something just because the rest of the rational world says it is correct.

Others would have looked on at Hannah not being able to get her darling Washerpop to move his feet, and looking in from the outside, they would have seen failure, but if you are learning something from the experience, then it is not a waste of time or a failure. Hannah was delighted to be shown how arse about face she had got things, and she felt humbled and proud that a horse she could have chosen to label "belligerent" in those moments had taught her something so valuable. Something that it would seem no human had been able to teach her, with all of their words and education and superiority.

Again, she marvelled at how equines have far more in common with humans than she ever thought: our complexities, our reasons for wanting and not wanting. Our base kindness and generosity, which like with you humans, can get undermined if fair exchange, physically and emotionally, does not take place and this does not need to be an outward physical thing such as a treat or praise. A reward for us, same as for you can be a mutual understanding in a moment, a give instead of a take.

My human was ecstatic to learn that I would only come riding with her if It really did please me, and very excited that I had shown her how to say no, and not give a gnat's poop about it.

CHAPTER 14

RESPONDING VERSUS REACTING

*When you react, you are giving away your power, when you respond,
you are staying in control of yourself. ~ Bob Proctor*

My human did, and a lot of you do, find having a horse who reacts
quickly to everything is a bit of a double-edged sword. You want us to
be quick to listen to you, quick off the leg; ready to stop in an
emergency situation and all those things. But you don't want us to be
ready to decide the barking dog means we should run home, or for us to
be quick to judge that the shadow in the corner of the arena has tigers
in it.

In wanting us to not react to things in a way that makes you feel
unstable on our backs you often let us know so firmly that you are
fearful of falling, that we go to the other extreme and decide that it
would be better for us not to move forward freely at all. We think you

want a shuffler, so we shuffle, so as not to wobble you off balance, and then you get on at us for shuffling.

My training of Hannah reminded her of something that happened when she was a child; she was sat quietly drawing a picture, it was very detailed and had taken her many hours to design, and she had nearly finished it. Hannah's sister came home and was rushing around the house, ranting because she was wanting to go out and could not find her favourite top that she wanted to wear; she must have that one to wear! On not being able to find it anywhere, she decided Hannah must have worn it and must still have it.

And so, she started to demand that Hannah should give her the top back, my human quietly stated that she never did have the top and does not have it now. This answer appeared to be the wrong one however, because her sister kept on at her about it still, getting louder and angrier. Hannah knew from previous experience that it was best to try to ignore her sister when she got irate like this! Upon not getting any answer from Hannah and getting more and more irate as her tantrum went unheeded and Hannah just continued to draw, this cross one snatched the drawing out of Hannah's hands, screwed the picture up into a ball, and threw it back at her sister. Hannah just looked at her and flipped her drawing pad to a fresh page, and without a word started the drawing over.

She had instinctively known as a youngster that not reacting was the best course of action if she did not want to get drawn into those negative feelings and experience that escalation of drama and indignation on both sides. She knew that if she was right about something (she had not taken the top) that she was perfectly within her own rights and moral code to ignore any drama pointed at her.

In fact, since Hannah has been hanging out with me she has been known to stick her fingers in her ears and sing; "la la la! I can't hear you" when faced with human moaning, whingeing and dramas. She gets told to grow up a lot. We both think this is hilarious.

On remembering how she used to do the same thing, Hannah began to understand when I would often just refuse to react to any stimulus; cajoling, pushing, pulling, I would keep my ears forwards and stay in my good feeling place, I was saying: "you join me here human, I am not going to join you in your rushing and demanding and fractious thoughts".

Only once Hannah had gone through her range of emotions and let go of her frustration towards me, and she was just standing there with a quiet mind, having thought every thought there was to think and having had to drop all of them because they were not getting her anywhere, would I say; "yes, now you are in a place where we can meet, now I will let you in, what was it you wanted again?"

Soon she began to drop the middle man of pushing her will onto mine and met me on equal terms to start with. This is the place where your intuition will guide you, this is how you respond, rather than to spend your whole life just reacting to external circumstance, this is how you can change your reality into one that is pleasing to you.

Believe it or not, you humans do have the ability to respond rather than react, remember that you are not reacting to a situation or person outside of you that is disagreeable; you are allowing a negative emotion inside of you (about the situation or person) to define your actions. In reacting, you are taking something as a personal affront, when in reality, anything another does to upset you is no reflection on who you are what so ever, it is a reflection of what is inside of them in that moment.

CHAPTER 15

DEEP IS NOT HEAVY

Dory: I shall call him Squishy and he shall be mine, and he shall be my Squishy. Come on, Squishy! Come on, little Squishy.

[baby talk, the jellyfish, stings her]

Dory: Ow! Bad Squishy, bad Squishy!

Finding Nemo, Disney.Pixar (2003)

Deep is light. We love it that more and more humans are wanting to deepen their connection and understanding with their equine friends, I showed Hannah that she had misplaced the real meaning of depth by adding to it a heaviness and seriousness that does not belong there. As our understanding of each other grew, she even wanted to change my name from Prince Washerpop to something more serious, profound and meaningful! Can you imagine, she could be shouting Aristotle or Socrates across the field to me and be expecting me to come running! I love my fun name, I am the one and only. In fact, I should say names, I do have quite a few more than Henry Bear of Cub Town, and he has plenty!

I came to Hannah known as Carlos but her friend at work misheard her and thought she said she had bought a horse called Carwash, everyone at Hannah's work would ask how Carwash was getting on, and so that name stuck. They would walk past her and sing that Rose Royce 'Carwash' song to her "talkin bout the car wash yeah!" and then she would come and sing it to me! My name evolved and got shortened to Wash, and then progressing to Washer, Washerpop, Prince Washerpop the 1st, Washeroo, Squasheroo, Squisharoo, Squishpie and Squishie, plain old Roo or Roosteroo. Oh and Washernoodlenoo.

The name on my passport says; Candor F. Hannah looked at my passport just recently after a very long time and realised for the first time, the significance of my passport given name.

Dictionary definition:

noun: candor

1.   the quality of being open and honest; frankness.

"a man of refreshing candour"

synonyms: frankness, openness, honesty, candidness, truthfulness, sincerity, forthrightness, directness, lack of restraint, straightforwardness, plain-spokenness, plain dealing, plainness, calling a spade a spade, unreservedness, bluffness, bluntness, outspokenness;

informal telling it like it is

Hannah thought, yep. That just about sums this one up. Washerpop calls a spade a spade alright. The "F" after Candor probably stands for "F**king bonkers" she thought. She did try to contact my breeder and previous owners in the Netherlands without much success. One reply she got, she put into Google translate and the only decipherable sentence of the conversation said; "He comes from the 'devil may care' breeder". Again, this made sense to my human. She thought that whoever this breeder was, it seems he was adventuring at splicing horse, shark, deer and alien DNA, and out popped this Washerpop, for she certainly had never met one like me before, I am such a mix of fabulous different things.

Deep does not mean turning your back on the lighter side of life.

Your young people know how to help you to remember this too, Hannah recently had a conversation with her six-year-old niece Hattie, who was sitting on Hannah's lap and needed to fart. Being such a lovely young girl, she got off of her auntie's lap, farted a few feet away and then climbed back up for cuddle time. Hannah's sister (Hattie's mum) laughed, and said: "You don't get off of my lap to fart, you just fart on me!" Shortly before that, there had been some upset when Hattie's father had told her she was not allowed to do a thing that she had wanted to do. Hattie now sat back on Hannah's lap and said; "we should never fight with each other because we are all one, so when we hurt another, we hurt ourselves as well". Hannah just stared at her beautiful young niece, mouth open, surprised and delighted to hear such clarity and wisdom coming from this little one! Hattie was asked if she learnt that at school, but she said it was just something that she knew to be true. Hannah said; "well Hattie, you are an amazing young lady; you blow me away with the things that you say!" Hattie replied; "I blow you away with my farts".

As I say, deep is not heavy, think of all of the marvellous creatures that live deep under the sea. Are they swimming around at the bottom of the ocean, saying "oh god" the depth is beautiful, this is where I want to be, this is where I have chosen to be, but my god it is heavy going down here! Every flap of my fin is such hard work!" no they do not, they are well suited to their environment, the depth is not heavy or burdensome to them, it is beautiful and natural.

The misunderstanding of depth of feeling can come as we strive to be more respectful of other beings wants, needs and wishes. We may see other humans who seemingly do not care deeply and have carelessness and reckless abandon around their animals, using names and stereotypes and trashy language about us, calling us opinionated or lazy or this or that. And those of you who have come to a deeper understanding want to put yourselves so far away from this kind of thing that you end up being very sombre about it all. Again, this is about grabbing hold of the opposite end of the stick; there is no balance there.

Hannah found that as she gravitated away from the people who did not understand her wanting to know us creatures more fully. And as she made friends with some who did hold a deeper regard for us, she found that there was a lot of seriousness going on, so much wanting to be mindful and develop something more, that all fun had gone completely out of the window!

Some of these ones who were seeking to give their animals more freedom of choice and to have a deeper regard for them found that their beasts were not overly keen to engage with them if there was to be no fun involved.

If you take life too seriously, the being respectful to us, to the point that you will not instigate, tolerate or join in any fun with us, then we are very likely to try to show you all the fun there is to be had. Most likely by making our own, probably in a way that is frustrating to you if you are not understanding this. When my human got very sombre about having a deeper respect and regard for me and my kind, do not get me wrong, I did and do appreciate this very much. But you humans can swing from one extreme to another; we may prefer the company of one who takes us out galloping and slings us back in the stable without a thought to getting us fit properly before or cooling us off afterwards, because they know how to have fun!

I would show Hannah when she got too serious about respecting me to the point that her feelings and any sense of humour went out of the window. We would go out riding, and I would try to roll in puddles, this got me a new name of Washer puddle duck. Sometimes she would want me to join her in meditation, and sometimes I would love this, but sometimes it was inappropriate timing for me if I was feeling cheeky and up for some fun. So I would bite her in the back of the knees and while she was off of her feet I would steal a shoe from one foot and run. It is fun to watch my human hobbling/hopping after me across the field shouting; "Washer Prince of Thieves! Bring my shoe back!"

The depth of understanding here comes from recognising when we want fun and when we want something else, just to be with you maybe; not for you to come to us with your prescribed hour a day or however long and you say, today I am going to be at one with my horse. You might want to bear in mind that today we might just want a bum scratch and that is as deep and meaningful as it is going to get.

You seem to be quite good at discerning that people have many facets, they have times when they want to go crazy, let off steam, or be by themselves or are in a contemplative state of mind, or are in a crappy mood and do not want cajoling out of that.

Can you see it is the same for us too? We have days, hours and moments where we are feeling in different moods and wanting to experience different things; nothing ever stays the same. Energy is fluid, you can change things to the same thing by bringing the same old thoughts with you, but that does not mean things aren't fluid or changing, it means things are changing to the same thing, you are getting the same old response from your outer world as the same old vibration you are projecting onto it.

Hannah knew quite early on with me that she was going to need to raise her game if she were not to always be three steps behind me, thinking wise, and therefore forever being caught on the hop. (Literally, so to speak when I stole her shoes) She would need to be able to adjust her thinking very quickly as I changed mine.

Part of fostering a deep connection with other beings is going with the flow, being open to adjusting your thought moment to moment to what you are receiving. If your horse comes to you and says, let's have some fun, and you hear that and say; ok! That is a deep connection and understanding, just right there; nothing more is needed in that moment.

CHAPTER 16

THOSE TRICKSY LITTLE HOBBITSES

Sam: What are you up to? Sneaking off, are we?

Gollum: Sneaking? Sneaking? Fat Hobbit is always so polite. Smeagol shows them secret ways that nobody else could find, and they say "sneak!" Sneak? Very nice friend. Oh, yes, my precious. Very nice, very nice.

Sam: All right, all right! You just startled me is all. What were you doing?

Gollum: Sneaking.

Lord of the Rings - Return of the King (2003)

Hannah often thought of how I seemed to have a view of humans that was much like Gollum's view of the tricksy hobbitses, and she would laugh, as I could be so indignant at other's behaviours but as tricksy and sneaky as I liked myself and completely unabashed in that too.

For months, when riding out with our one horse/human combination who would come with us, I would sneak up to this horse and if I thought my human's eye was not on the ball, I would leap and try to mount him! He would jump forwards away from me, at the same time as Hannah would haul my head around to try to get me off of him. Often, by the time the rider of this horse had looked behind to see what had made him jump, Hannah had got me a few feet away, and we would both be staring off into the trees, hannah whistling a random tune... 'Nothing to see here!'

To this day this lady still does not know what I was up to, she would have been horrified to know, and would not have accompanied us on rides anymore, so Hannah was all for keeping these little incidents quiet.

After months of me larking around in this manner, and this horse and rider being decidedly fabulous in escorting us and showing me how to calmly and sensibly cope with traffic, and herds of deer and children with balloons, and everything in between; one fabulously sunny summer morning, we were going for a fantastic side by side canter along the ridge of a very tall hill, I felt like king of the world up there. Hannah was thinking, my goodness, this is the life! as I for once kept an excellent steady pace alongside my friend, the sun beating down, breath-taking views all around; you could see for miles and miles up here!

And then half way along the ridge, there was a small tree with a few cows laying down under there, our companion horse, saw them and just did a little body swerve away from them as we cantered past, but as he did, he bumped into me! I stopped dead! So quickly I nearly head butting my human in the face. The other horse and rider continued cantering along the track, as I stood, (past the cows by this time) Hannah used her legs to ask me forward again, but my answer was; "BUT HE BUMPED ME!!!" I was so indignant that I decided to go home.

It took a lot for Hannah to persuade me otherwise, the other rider by this time had stopped way up the track and is shouting back to us; "is he scared of the cows?"

I did not give a jot about those cows and Hannah did not have the energy or the inclination to explain the truth; that I was outraged to have been bumped and was not going riding with THAT horse that BUMPED me anymore! Hannah thought, not for the first time how I was as tricksey as hell, while all the time indignant at what I perceived as others tricksiness.

Hannah knew from the time she accidentally gave me a static electric shock on the nose, and I would not come anywhere near her for three weeks, that I did not know what an 'accident' was. I always concluded that there was deviousness and conniving going on against Prince Washerpop and that I must always be wary of these tricksy ones with their tricksy ways.

I could be so indignant and resistant to things. And when I say things, it was very confusing for Hannah, because it wasn't always the same stuff I didn't like or want to do, I could be very enthusiastic about something one day and do a complete u-turn in my opinion on the subject the next day. Even just going out to the field, some days I just wanted to stay indoors and not even look out over my stable door. Hannah could muck out and do my hay and water with the door open, and I would try to make myself invisible, in case she wanted to try to turn me out into the field. She thought she could trick me out with handfuls of treats along the way, I would do one step and stop, much cajoling would take place, half way there I would most often turn around and drag my human back to the stable. All Hannah knew at the beginning of this is that I had problems and that she didn't want to look at them, it felt too uncomfortable because she did not know how to resolve them. Maybe they would just disappear if she just kept on loving me.

While this way of going at things was partly right, in that there was no point in focusing on something that she couldn't see a way of changing,

Hannah knew that while doing all the things that we could achieve, she was not working on some things that were important to her. Like me not wanting to walk next to a human or me not wanting to have my legs and feet touched. Thinking every new thing we tried was maybe going to be a trick, and on finding it wasn't, just deciding it didn't rock my boat and I didn't want to do it anyway! I had previously learned that if I happily go along with the human, to begin with, then I may find myself in a position which I did not sign up for.

As a youngster I got tricked into small spaces where the humans forced me into two choices; compromise or defend myself. If you escalate, in being the human boss and needing for the horse to be submissive, he may have a variety of different tactics to deal with that, but my point is, if you get him to go along with you under duress, he will feel tricked. I went along with those humans; we take you at face value assuming your inbuilt natural humanity before we know better, we take you at your word, YES AT YOUR WORD. And the humans did not say; "I will ask you nicely and if you do not do as asked I will force you to do it". They said; "you can trust us Candor, we are kind and friendly" so I went with them, and then when I did not willingly do as they desired, I got forced. This is crucial and something that most people training horses do not realise about us; we DO take you entirely at your word! (to begin with, until you have repeatedly shown your word is not to be trusted) But when something ceases to be fun for a horse, because it is boring or difficult, or physically painful or not understandable to him as to why he should be doing it, and he doesn't want to continue because of that, he feels tricked into the situation if you then force it. It is like inviting some friends for a picnic and then serving them up dog shit sandwiches.

No amount of enthusiastic praise; "good boys" or "well done's" or pats on the neck are going to make your friends like eating those sandwiches.

CHAPTER 17

LEADERSHIP – ANOTHER WAY

I start with the premise that the function of leadership is to produce more leaders, not more followers. ~ Ralph Nader

All of us want to be the chosen ones, we all want to be made to feel special, and unless somethings have caused us feel very jaded in life, we also want to make others that we love feel special too. There are lots of chapters in this book explaining lots of different parts to this some of which overlap, but the biggest thing overall that I have taught Hannah, by showing her this in myself is that to be the chosen one, you first have to choose yourself. You have to opt to put yourself before others, and that by being selfish you can ultimately become selfless, not easy to get your tiny humans brains around, I know!

To be selfish in this manner means not to feel bad to want what you want, even if that flies in the face of what is standard or what others around you believe is right for you. You want to be caring so much about your own wellbeing and feelings that you do not allow anything to derail you of off your track. Once you have chosen yourself, you will become the calm, confident fun person you would like to be, and your equine partner WILL then choose you. Choose you to dance with, you to laze with on a Sunday afternoon, opt to have a joke with you, choose to ask you when uncertain of what to do. Ultimate bliss lays here.

If you do not know how to make yourself happy how do you think another should be willing to follow your guidance on anything in life?

That would be to follow someone who does not have faith that the world is a beautiful place, no belief that they have the power within to make things great, so they have to force things into a shape they call happiness, it makes no sense to follow one who is like this.

I showed Hannah by NEVER for one minute conceding to a human unless my stand point on it got considered. I kept myself whole, not flinching at the thought of punishment, I did not allow any parts of me to be diminished or taken away, knowing I could not hold onto my inner peace and happiness by allowing my soul to get slowly chipped away.

Once my human began to understand this is what I felt and it is at the heart of my being, then my heart swelled with joy, and the real dance could begin.

Hannah tried to learn how best to get to grips with a horse who thinks he is right and the human is wrong in most subjects, and who also appeared not to have noticed he was a castrated male. I would mount boy and girl horses and be dominant with people and equines alike. Hannah started to look at different ways of training; they had to be in line with her expanding ethics, she sought out different trainers doing different things. But although she learned bits and pieces from them that were helpful, it always came down to the same thing with a lot of these methods; they always came back to needing the human to be dominant over the horse. Needing to show them how it is (usually explained as natural herd behaviour!) and Hannah was so at odds with this one, she had to find out why.

For starters, any kind of trying to show me; Prince Washerpop the 1st, that you the human were the herd leader went down like a lead balloon; I would either ignore my lovely human or bite her in the head. With a big smile, of course, a bit of a crocodile smile! Hannah could have endlessly chased me in circles to assert her dominance as a herd leader, but doing that does not create a leader in you!

If Hannah were to chase me away until I decide my best course of action for my survival is to concede to the human and stop running, then that has nothing to do with me respecting the human or seeing her as my true leader! It has to do with me conceding to her because it is the best thing I can do for myself at that moment. Conceding would be a survival tactic, not a bonding as you ones have been told!

Try chasing your horse off in an open space and see how quick he comes back to you! Given a choice the horse does not bond/connect/gain respect for a human who takes this course. Although you may think that is what you are seeing on the surface of it, and yes you can condition us this way, but it has little to do with allowing us the autonomy from which real conversation and understanding can flow.

The same principle is there with this other one Hannah was always hearing; it is ok to use the whip or admonish the horse if you do it without anger if you do it just to show you are in charge, or to move the horse forward or away. Again Hannah would see this done to other horses and she would see them comply with what the human wanted but in a very shut down way. Nothing about creating a partnership here, all about the horse taking the best course of action for his survival at that moment, and then acquiescing until they can be out of the situation; creating robot reactions instead of pure responses. Where is the joy in that? Where is the harmony? Because horses are big animals, people think they are justified in being kind up until a point, and then there is a point where defensiveness, fearfulness and reprimand are acceptable.

So, if you think that your horse needs to learn that you are a good leader through various methods of chasing him around, chastising or getting on at him, what if he does not consider you to be a good leader because you have continued to work him when he has shown you with his behaviour that he is not ready for that? Or if you have constantly ignored him when he has shown you he is stressed by how he is being viewed and addressed by you? How then is he to see you as a good leader?

What do you deem to be good manners? Generally, for your horses, you consider good manners along a line of what's taught is good manners for humans. You see us as your children. They must learn to be well behaved in front of others, not to bite. Hannah bit quite a few people as a kid – dentists, hairdressers and doctors giving inoculations. She knew she would be hypocritical to get on at me about that. We must not be bargy or pushy, or we may physically injure a human and it will be all the person's fault because they never taught that horse any manners!

A day came when it was shown to Hannah that I did trust her to lead, but that in fact most of the time, being a leader myself, I was never going to follow blindly. She had previously noted that this was the case with me with other horses too, I could be seen out in the field charging around here and there by myself, and not moving an inch on occasion when something scared the herd into action that had not bothered me at all. I would not go with them "just because". Most people have trouble handling me at all on the ground, anyone watching Hannah handle me would say she is incompetent at best, as I go off wherever I feel like, I bite, I plant my feet, I break free.

The only reason my sweet human plucked up the courage to first get on my back was because she knew however bad riding me turned out to be, it could not possibly be worse than trying to deal with me on the ground, and she was right.

On this one particular day out riding, something happened to properly scare me, a very calm, uneventful ride changed dramatically at the top of a big hill. There are a lot of big hills here in the Chilterns, our stable yard at the time was nestled in a bit of a valley, so we mostly ended up coming home down a hill.

I suddenly panicked and I started to run and buck down this steep incline. Each time I bucked Hannah was getting a little further thrown out of the saddle, she would manage to slow me to a walk and stroke my neck, offering some soothing words, only for me to leap, zoom off and start bucking again.

It didn't look as though I was about to calm down about things anytime soon, and Hannah could not see anything around us that may have set me off, although she did know I had exceptional hearing and may be able to hear something that she could not.

The lady we were riding with was getting very upset, and was saying to Hannah; "please get off, you are going to fall off, so please get off before that happens". Now Hannah knew this woman was talking sense, but she really very much did not want to get off of my back, because she knew I was harder to deal with on the ground than in the saddle and I was already out of control of my feelings and actions.

Against her better judgement, Hannah got off of my back, as she was close to getting catapulted off anyway. She was trying to calm me on the ground, but I just continued to leap and buck, the same as when Hannah was on my back. Unknown to both of us at the time, I had a physical illness that had affected my nervous system I was completely unable to calm down, I could not see or hear properly, and all my nerve endings felt as though they were on fire.

We headed towards home, Hannah trying to walk as calmly as she could by my side as I leapt about alongside her, dragging her off into the bushes; it was over a mile to get back home, mostly downhill on very narrow tracks through woodland. Hannah had no idea what was wrong with me and could only think on getting us home safely.

She talked to me the whole time and she managed to ring ahead and ask a friend at the stable yard to come out; she was worried that she might have a loose horse heading across the main road if she could not keep a hold of me.

Hannah was petrified but determined to get us safely home. She had no choice but to put herself in the hands of the gods, as I leapt and bronked above her head on these narrow paths scattering dog walkers and cyclists as we went.

Then we came to an extremely narrow path, less than a foot wide, Hannah would have to go in front of me, she did not want to walk in front of a horse who had apparently lost his mind and thought his feet were plugged into the mains electricity, but there was no choice.

I could not see or hear properly and I could not control the freakish energy zooming through my body. Do you know what I did? I grabbed Hannah's coat in my teeth, just on her shoulder, I was so frightened, and I couldn't make out what shapes were in the shadows of the trees, so I held onto her shoulder and followed where she went. Hannah could feel me behind her doing little leaps and bucks hardly able to contain myself, and do you know what? We walked all the way home like this. Trust that when it matters your horse will not hurt you, he will, in fact, do everything in his power not to. So long as you have been offering kindness and understanding and consideration for his feelings. You cannot provide those things to another if you have not already previously consistently chosen them for yourself. Deep down, you people know this, that is why we try to seek it out of you, we know that you know it.

Hannah did not try to control my out of control-ness with dominance; she had already decided to choose kindness and understanding for herself, I followed her because I knew she had that to give to another.

Before this leaping episode, when I was feeling very well, it was late autumn and we had gone out on a ride on such a ludicrously windy day! There had been a storm the night before with weather warnings and trees blown down, the next morning the wind had only eased a little, and others at the stable yard told Hannah and the two ladies she was with that they were stark raving mad to be going out riding in the woods. But my fabulous girls were not getting as much chance to have these long rides in the woods with it getting dark early in the evenings, and they had booked a morning off of work, they very much wanted to take us horses out and trusted that all would be well.

At this stage in my riding, Hannah was still relying on the other riders we went out with to lead the way, allowing me to follow until I got more experience and a bit braver about things. On this day, there were a few trees down along our way, we managed to sidle around them on the wider tracks until we got right up into the woods, and we were on a very narrow track that gradually turns into a bit of a ravine. We had steep sides left and right, and as we turned a corner there was a big old tree fallen in the storm and blocking our path.

It looked unpassable as the tree straddled the deep ditch like track we were travelling along, my Hannah and the second lady were saying; "it is a shame, but we will have to turn around and go back the way we came". The third lady, however, was a very experienced event rider, and she thought it looked like we could go up the right-hand side of the gulley, along a short little bit of track and back down the other side. Just as Hannah and the second lady started to protest that they thought we should play it safe and turn back, I Washerpop, barged past my companions and stomped straight up the side of this ravine. I stepped very carefully along the top narrow edge, while Hannah leant right down over my neck so as not to have her head whipped off by the very low hanging branches. And then I popped myself down the other side, I turned and waited to see my friends follow. Hannah had never been so proud in all of her life; for all of the times I could be mistrusting of situations, this time I had listened to the humans disagreeing about proceeding or turning back and I assessed this one. I didn't want to go back and I knew I could do it, so I took matters into my own hands before anyone had a chance to protest.

My human could have protested and tried to turn me back, not that there was really any time or space to do that, so quick was my decision and it was such a small area we were stuck in. She felt so exhilarated that despite a lot of her own kind telling her around this time that unless she took me in hand, things would not end well for us; despite this she knew and I had just shown her that I had an excellent ability to understanding things. I knew my own capabilities, and I had complete faith in my own decision-making skills.

My adorable human; by being a good leader (even though she looked to be the opposite in most people's eyes) and by not defining leadership as bossing or telling or giving of instructions, had created another leader, not a robotic follower. She was delighted at these glimpses of pure alignment between us when they happened, how marvellous to have a partnership where either one can take the helm as and when they feel happy to step up to the mark.

This is the kind of give and take we both wanted, on returning to the stable yard, Hannah with a grin like the Cheshire cat, telling of her brave, powerful and wise Washerpop fearlessly tackling our own Derby bank, did not care for once about the other human's lack of enthusiasm at our endeavours. She knew now that we were building something special for ourselves, she did not need others to understand or praise, she knew we understood each other and that was all that mattered.

CHAPTER 18

BEING AND DOING

'Tain't what you do (It's the way that you do it) ~ Ella Fitzgerald 1939

As you squishy old humans progress and evolve into wanting an equal partnership; a friendship where both can give and take unconditionally, I think you nearly all seem to go through a phase of struggling with what/how much is it fair to do with your horse, is it fair to ride? Is it reasonable or necessary to put a bit in our mouths? Is it fair to do anything at all but to leave us roaming in the pasture?

You look to different people's approaches to see what it is that they have decided is best for us, and this is missing the point. I would like you to know something; we don't come here to this planet in a horse body to get freed from martyrdom by you. We are aware when we get here that we have chosen to experience the contrast too, like you; I could not appreciate the sun on my back if I did not have the opposite of that with which to compare. And I have said to you at the start of this book that we do not need to get given perfect conditions to be able to live a happy life.

We learn and know what we like and what is not to like, we have come too, to learn and expand, just like you. We are aware of our true selves more easily than you humans are, and know what we want and need to be happy much more readily than you do because we are not taught so much, as youngsters, as you are, how to socially conform. We can enjoy the moment more, for not having too many thoughts about the past and the future as you do, this is how we give you feedback in the moment of what we are liking and not liking about what is occurring with us. This is why we want you all to be more present in the moment with us. I would often shut myself off completely from Hannah when she came to Henry and I with a head full of worries; tight as a coiled spring, wanting softness and openness from us and wondering why we could not meet her there, the way that she was.

Your only job and your only rules are just to be guided by what we show you in the moment and to respond by adjusting something within yourself to change an undesired behaviour or attitude from us, into what you do desire. Become sensitive enough to yours and our feelings, so that you can feel us in the moment and make a change there and then. This is how you can progress from just "being" to "doing". This is how you will know if we actually are enjoying having you on our backs and learning your human tricks; by being in tune enough and caring enough about how we feel to only do and only go at a pace where we can feel happy and confident.

Hannah felt such a joyous skip in her heart, the first couple of times that she finished what we were doing and I said; "hey, I am having a ball, let us do some more!" instead of me just tolerating her, or getting annoyed with her asking in the wrong way, over and over again.

We need to understand your requests and to not feel compromised by going along with them, of course, you will see people who get us to do things under coercion and with force. If you are anything like Hannah you will have wondered more than once why we horses put up with such things when you see that dressage horse with his neck bent and forced into his chest. Because we live more in the moment, we will always give you the chance, moment to moment to hear what we are telling you. You have an opportunity in every moment to get it right, to listen to us, instead of beating that old drum of; "listen to me, listen to me, listen to me."

It's a very human thing also, to want to rescue or want to be saved; you watch films where ladies get swept away by knights in shining armour, you have "Goodies" and "Baddies" that go through some sort of conflict or battle and then the goodies usually win. We do not view life in those terms; we would never be waiting for something better to come along down the line. But that doesn't mean we enjoy or want negativity any more than you do, but we know that we can only know what we want by experiencing what we don't want, we are feeling our way through life too.

And we will always show our humans when we want or need something different from them, sometimes, as you know; people are not ready to listen because they are too busy listening to what they have been taught and think they already know about what you do with horses.

We do not usually come from a place of anger or retaliation this is because we are aware that the only way to bring love to ourselves, is to show love. We know we are love, most of you humans are not aware of this, those who are unable to show love and compassion have not been shown it enough themselves, this is why we continue to give love even if it is not always returned.

You know punishment does not work, or your prisons would not be full up, but still, you often do not want to be the ones to be proactive, to show up with love and compassion. You want an instructor to sort your horse out, you want your government to do something about the problems in your society, you do not yet know that the answer lies within you and starts with love.

The only way for us to get through your human preconditioning, your thoughts of: "I must make my horse do this, this and this" is to show you love back, this is not weakness or stupid-ness, it is because we never give up on you being able to love back. Because you have been brought up to believe in such an achieving, goal orientated world; the world where you all are judged not to be enough just as you are. You can put that judgement onto your horse. Time and time again we say to you "no – not like this; like this!" we will always show you when you have got it right for us, or not! always. And this compassion we prove to you, moment after moment, remember, you also have an unlimited supply of love, it is only your conditioning that makes you believe that you need to ration it out when deserved.

People readily judge and condemn others who are yet to reach the higher place of understanding that think they have got to. This attitude is detrimental to humans progressing further in their thinking. Because that thought of 'those ones, over there; doing wrong', comes from the same conditioned/conditional place as the view of; "make the animal do this thing to serve my purpose".

Again, it is conditional love; 'I will love you if you behave in a way I find acceptable', that kind of thought does not come from a place of love. You can only teach and show your fellow humans from a place of love, from a place of showing by example that you can be unconditional and non-judgemental. You need to be the experience you wish to pass on.

That is what I Prince Washerpop am; I am 100% passing on of my infinite love, I know it to be so. Looking at someone who you believe to be unkind to their animals and saying they should not do that or that you think that they should get punished, is the same as sending your 3-year-old to jail for not being able to solve a complicated math problem. If that person has never been shown this love or experienced it, he has no capability to show it to others! If you can understand this you will know true compassion; it will open up your life and not just with your horses.

It is absolutely possible do 'be and do' if you stay in the moment and keep an open heart.

CHAPTER 19

UNCONDITIONAL LOVE

Even after all this time, The Sun never says to the earth, "you owe me".
Look what happens with a love like that, It lights up the whole sky. ~
Hafiz

Sorry but you humans DO need this one spelling out, unconditional love is being happy, confident and secure enough in yourself that your happiness is enhanced by interactions with your loved ones. Only then is your happiness coming from within you and you will stop trying to get others to behave in a way to induce your happiness.

Conditional love is when someone else in your life has to behave in a certain way for you to be happy. For example; you may not say "jump this scary water jump, or it is off to the knackers yard for you". You may not even mean anything part way towards that extreme, but every time we do something against your wishes and feel your disappointment or frustration you are saying to us: You are not good enough as you are. You will be good enough once your behaviour pleases me, then I will love you so.

How long would you stick with a boyfriend/girlfriend/husband/wife or friend, who, when you are trying to lose weight, got cross at you, or sighed and looked at you with disappointment in their eyes if you picked up a biscuit? How bad does that kind of thing make you feel about yourself? And more importantly; how much does that make you want to give up trying? What are your first thoughts in a situation like this? I DO NOT LIKE PEOPLE THAT I LOVE TELLING ME HOW I SHOULD BE! and who on earth do they think they are? Perfect themselves?

Most humans are a bit confused about what unconditional love means, you think it means putting up with rubbish from others, compromising yourself and your own needs, selling out on your unique, legitimate, inner being, inner code, but it is not that at all, it is the opposite in fact; you must begin to feel able to stand in celebration of your uniqueness, to be able to say to another; "yes your view is different than mine, but I am so strongly comfortable in my own skin, your view being different to mine is not a threat to me, I do not need to try to change you or your opinions to keep my equilibrium; I can still have love for you".

You seem to know that you mostly find it easier to love your animals than your fellow humans because you understand that your animals do show you unconditional love. You define this as us not caring if you have brushed your hair or not, or if you are wearing odd socks, or do not drive a brand new shiny car, that kind of thing.

But it is more than that, we beasts do not give our love from a cynical or fear based point of view, we give it freely because we have not been taught to ration it out like you, and because we live more in the present moment, we are able to love without that love being coloured so much by past events or future possible outcomes, and although you love that we love unconditionally, you are very rarely able to return us the compliment, because you do love us less if we behave in ways that are unbefitting.

Hannah had just been going along like most humans do; trying to be kind to the ones you love while still feeling good about the relationship yourselves. But this never worked out for her, she would still feel hurt, particularly by disagreements with other humans and she would still shut herself off from love as a form of protection. She never felt right when that anxious pained look came across my face, that look that said; "you are not seeing me in this moment. And I am anxious because once you stop seeing me, you humans start trying to force your way through a problem, and that never works out very well for me."

She knew unconditional love meant what it says on the tin, but she didn't know how to achieve that. What is that balance between being so sweet and getting walked all over or being too controlling or wanting things to be perfect? If you think about it, you do know trying to control others doesn't work, you see with your young people often, that telling them not to do something is all that is required to make them go and do it.

You humans, not having much clarity of thought, and distracting yourselves from ever finding any, with TV, alcohol and anything else you can find, to put off looking at yourselves; You mostly believe you must compromise in relationships, you also think us equines should compromise our moral standings to align with your preferences.

It is easy to think that you are an unconditionally loving being when things are going well, and life is going pretty easy on you, and then when there is a problem, you either try to ignore it (distract yourselves) or go at it hammer and tongs. Opposite ends of the stick, when what you need is in the middle.

It is only when things get hard that you find out who you are.

Hannah thought ok; "I will just be as good a person as I can" but she found this didn't stop things from occurring that she didn't want in her reality. She thought she unconditionally loved me and others; she would look at Henry and I every day and see our beautiful spirits, our mere presence in her life filling her heart with joy. And that is what it is all about, but then she would still go on to need us to do things to please her, and then judge us on the results.

Even if you are doing what you do, believing it is for the good of another, you can still be very conditional. Of course, Hannah thought she was right to tell me not to eat lightbulbs, but if telling me that means she will judge me to be whole, and acceptable when I stop doing that thing, and therefore not love me as I am right now, then she, like all of you, is going to get more of what you don't want from us animals and your children.

I base my decisions on what pleases me. Remarkably, Hannah thought, I would often keep my cool if other horses on our ride were over excitable. It pleased me to not join in the circus on some occasions; this also pleased Hannah very much. But it made her see; she could not pigeon hole me, I was not one thing, I could be spooky, I could be the calmest one, I could be reckless, I could be responsible, I could be lazy or on fire.

For a long time, she did not know how to train me because I did not fit one defined group. Until one day she recognised quite how much I based whether or not I would go along with things on whether it made me happy or not! Such a novel idea for you humans, it still makes me laugh. Honestly, it was like my dear little person had discovered that the earth was not flat! to know I knew I had a god given right to be on this planet and please myself! Halleluiah!

Ah, and I know what you humans will always say about that; 'well that is all very well so long as beings are not doing just as they please and hurting others in the process' and you say that, being sure in your knowledge that there are people out there who do as they please and very much hurt other beings, so how could you be wrong in that statement?

Because the answer to those who do things that are undesirable, uncaring or even abhorrent, is not to punish, ostracise or banish them. They would not be doing those things to begin with if they knew, because they had been shown some of it: what unconditional love is.

Do not get caught up thinking; Yes, I have learnt this concept, I understand what unconditional love is, so now I understand it, I have it. NO you do not.

Having an open heart, approaching every being and your planet with love, and not losing sight of that love when something or someone challenges you, is a moment to moment thing. You will need to do as us beasts naturally do, and choose every day, minute and second, to come from a place of love, until it becomes natural for you again.

Someone will always get your goat, your responsibility to yourself here is to let that go as quickly as possible, and choose love, when the option is there for you to go either way.

Also, your need for us to love or like you back causes many problems for you.

If you have been tirelessly efforting on our behalf to look after us and train us, and then one day when the grass is just too lush and tempting, and we turn our back to you when you come out to the field with a halter, you get a bad feeling inside about us. You want us to put you above all else; you think this will mean that we love you back.

Humans have this very funny idea, they think that feeling and showing an abundance of love to another means you can expect something in return from that one. An investment must show a return to be worthy, like with your finances.

The only way you will get the return you seek is to happily give all of yourself, all of the love you have to give, without one thought of what your gain will be, without expectation that the other will, or should, evenly match your input.

Love is not a competition, it is not the stock exchange! choosing to limit the love you are willing to show because another has offended your senses, or seemingly not matched your input, will stuff you up every single time.

CHAPTER 20

LETTING GO OF CONTROL

Remember, licking doorknobs is illegal on other planets. ~ Spongebob
Squarepants

Letting go of control was the last thing for Hannah to be able to do completely, ooh, she did hold on to the illusion of control, the little vestiges she had of it, as tightly as she could for as long as she could.

We really have no control in life because we do not have control over how other people or beings feel, or ultimately what they will do, the only control we can have, is how we respond or react to external influences. Trying to control each other's behaviour will always lead to more frustration for you and more resistance from the other party.

As you have read through my book, you may have made some links between what we have been talking about and how you feel about things. If you have resonance and wish to tune yourself this way also, please remember, it is not an instantaneous thing for you humans (or us either) to be able to change everything we are doing overnight, do it a little bit at a time.

Another last straw for Hannah was when she was wanting to trimming our feet one day; I refuse to be tied to anything, I stay put when I choose to, quite often I would break loose and just stay where I was untied, to prove the point that it should be my choice, not because I wanted to go somewhere else.

So, I stay loose and free for the task of hoof trimming unless Hannah has another human to help. She does not often get herself another human to help, because I usually bite them a lot and then break loose from them and then they do not want to come and help again.

It was not just because of my behaviour that Hannah did not look forward to trimming our feet, Henry Bear has pretty much been a darling angel all of his life about things like this, but now he is not liking lifting and having his legs held up so much as his joints are a bit creaky and stiff, it hurts him to bend and hold a leg in any one position, so trimming his feet was not an easy task either.

I used to be very stompy and did not want you, humans, to pick up my feet without permission, but I am accepting this now if Hannah asks permission and does not judge my behaviour, and if I do not have my Golem head on, some days it does not matter what you humans do, I am still on the lookout for your tricksey-ness.

Sometimes my human has to allow me to pick up her feet with my teeth first, if she does not allow this, I will not allow her to lift mine from the ground. I was delighted on this particular occasion that Hannah had decided the best course of action would be to bribe us boys with haylage. Henry likes haylage well enough, but me, oh boy! it is ALL about the haylage, I love, love, love it! Hannah watches as I go into a blissful trance while eating this stuff, she calls it Washer catnip, she thinks she could probably get a chainsaw and chop me into little bits whilst I munch on haylage, and I would still have my om nom nom nom face on, my eyeballs rolled back in my head, I am totally blissed out.

My human could not believe how easy I was to do on this occasion, no fuss or resistance, and in no time at all, she had my fronts done, and made a start on Henrys, but Mr H Bear made a run for it half way through one foot and had to be put on a halter and be tied up! I thought this was highly amusing and tried to help, I chewed on the Bears head, and then I got told to go away, my help was not wanted!

Hannah thought Henry was being very impatient and very fussy about having his feet done and because he has always been excellent about foot trimming in the past, Hannah took this as a personal insult. Henry kicked out (ever so lightly) and got a proper telling off, she had wrenched her back now, and was getting cross that things were not going well, but she was determined to get finished. Then when she was lifting a hind hoof, Henry managed to secretly untie himself (He undid the knot in the rope with his teeth, he is sneaky too sometimes!) and as Hannah let his hind leg back to the ground, and he cautiously tiptoed off, I thought I would help by galloping past him and taking us both off up the hill.

Hannah slumped down onto on the ground defeated, with a sore back and less than one of Henry's hoofers trimmed. She sat there and looked at us up on the hill, she knew how unfair she had been to demand that Henry is well behaved just because he always had been. Just because she felt she could not cope with two wild beasts, did not give her the right to have differing standards for Bear and I. She felt ashamed that she had taken such trouble over making sure she came to me with the right attitude; calmness patience and an acceptance that we would go at a pace I was comfortable with, and then she had just ridden roughshod all over Henry Bears feelings when he had given her so very much in life.

Then she laughed, as she thought how much I had rubbed off onto Henry, he may have been prepared to put up with discomfort to please the human in the past, but seeing that I never would and that Hannah had to bend to me, made Mr Bear stand up for himself! Yes! Hannah laughed and clapped her hands, she walked to us, up the hill, and hugged us both and thanked Henry for showing her and praised his courage to say no.

She made a promise to him there and then, to give him every ounce of consideration that she gave to me – the difficult one, who was now easy! She always encourages Henry Bear to demand to see her kindest most loving self now. And now, he is patient and allows her his feet, she is as gentle as can be with those joints that can hurt if moved the wrong way.

This realization that she had been treating us unequally, going out of her way to make me feel accepted and at ease, but just expecting Henry to be as he always had been; the amenable, pliable well behaved one, gave her the answer to a question that she had desperately been looking for somewhere else. (have you noticed that? If you lose your keys and look for them but can't find them, but then misplace something else, look for the something else, and strangely, you find your keys! This is because you took your negative focus off of the first problem, and then it got answered for you)

From when I first came to Hannah, she had viewed the relationship I have with Henry Bum Fluff as faulty, she thought I could be bullying and rough with him and she felt worse about this when it ended up being just the two of us together in the field, no other horses to share out the burden of the unwanted attention I gave.

She blamed herself for bringing crackpot old me along and felt that Henry, in his old age, did not need Washer the armpit biter, endlessly trolling him around the field. She knew by now that the answer was not to look at the problem with angst, but of all the things she had been successful in doing that, she found it very hard not to feel guilty when looking at her big old generous Henry Bear.

She kind of did know at times that all was well really between us two because if she tried to separate us even for a minute we would go nuts about that, Henry more so than me! not the actions of two who hate each other. And she did have an idea that I Washerpop only got on at H Bear at feeding times, so of course Hannah saw this the most.

She also saw, that I would shovel my food down my gullet as quickly as I could, and then go to steal Henry's, but on the very rare occasion that Henry was actually a bit hungry or cold, he did stand his ground and say no to me sharing. She realized; he is not weakly and helplessly letting Washer have his food, that kind and generous Bear will always share unless he really needs it for himself.

I keep my weight on very well over the winter months, and Bear does not, but even then, he knows when he does and doesn't want/need that food, he does not need a human to decide that for him. I take his, not because I need it, but because there was not enough when I was younger, I got used to taking all I can when I can, for myself, not knowing when more would be available, Henry Bear has always known there is enough for all.

So, what happened with Bear saying a big fat NO to Hannah on that day of hoof trimming, was two things. I love my Brother Bear, but I did not like him being a big old sucky-suck ass to the humans, as you can imagine, completely against my theology!

He gained massive respect in my eyes that day he said no to Hannah's demanding and kicked out at her, I saw something I had not seen in him before and I liked it! That's why I took him for a celebration gallop up the hill, we were like those Scots in the film Braveheart; Freeeeeedom!

The second thing was that my lovely human was able to shift her perspective of him at long last; from one of feeling guilty at having inflicted me onto him, of seeing him as old and not robust, she had forgotten how robust this beautiful big boy was and still is! She had forgotten what a fab sense of humour he had until he kicked out at her and then knobbed off up the hill with me; brothers in arms! She shifted back to seeing him as whole too, not needing defending or feeling sorry for, she also knew what a disservice she had done him by expecting him to deal with whatever she chucked at him, without coming to him with the mindfulness she came to me with, she did not do that to me, as I would not allow it, and she should not have done it to Henry just because he had put up with it before.

Hannah was not altogether unsurprised, when after this shift in her, she saw us getting on much better too, Henry grouched at me at dinner time! Go grouchy bear, Go! He had taken back his power, and she had a tear in her eye, the day she was grooming us both, and as usual, I would have a bit of an attempt to groom Mr Henry B. Henry would usually shift his body out of reach the second my teeth got within range of his bum, but this time he stayed, and I had a little practice at grooming Henrys butt! Hannah had said; gently please Washerpop, and gently I went.

The first successful interaction of my teeth with Henry's bum in three years! No wonder my human cried those happy tears! I was secretly chuffed to bits, but as usual I had to appear to the human like it was no big deal. Henry was as surprised at himself to be able to have a different reaction to my advances too!

This control may seem to be the hardest thing to let go of because you could tell everyone in the world, that you chastised your horse for almost kicking you and not patiently standing for a foot trim, and hardly a person would tell you that what you did was unjustified. But at that moment as Hannah had sat on the ground, instead of judging herself by other's values, and therefore justifying her harshness with Bear, she felt mortified that she had punished the one who had never put a foot wrong all of his life, for one misdemeanour. Instead of admitting she had no right to demand from this one, just because he didn't usually brutally object like I Washerpop did.

Only when she let go of needing to control and let go of her frustration over things she could not control, could either of us meet her in the place where she wanted to be met. How can we be open to calmly accepting and acquiescing to what you are wanting from us if you say it has to be this one way only, this way that you have set yourself on? Your way or the highway.

Hannah never thought in a million years that I would be good for Henry as I had been so good for her, and she did not mind one bit that our bonding on that day was in our agreement that the human needed to get that great big self-righteous stick out from up her arse.

CHAPTER 21

HUMILITY

If you are irritated by every rub how will you be polished? - Rumi

This Rumi quote has come to mean a great deal to my human. I rubbed and rubbed, and she did not want polishing! You people grow up being taught to ignore or push through your emotions, instead of acknowledging them and letting them go, and you try to push this way of thinking onto us. If you get upset about every little thing, just because you can, just because you may be right about that thing, then you will spend the rest of your life doing just that, noticing what is wrong in life, and getting irked by it.

Humility means never judging yourself as better than others and therefore never having an opinion that you have a right to force upon another. A hard habit to break when most of western society hinges on this, thin people being better than fat people! Rich people being more intelligent and having supposedly tried harder in life than poor people! And it goes on and on. And in our case, your perceived horse/person hierarchy, what do you really believe here? Do you feel we need you to be our herd leaders? Or do you want us to be your friends?

Do you think for such large and sometimes unpredictable animals we need to defer to the human when they ask because we have no idea of what kind of trouble we could get you both into? You know how we annoy you by refusing to be caught, not picking up a foot or spooking in the arena? Do you know that you continue that by being irked and not letting go of that negative emotion? Needing to be right and having humility do not go together well they have different vibrations.

This all may sound like a massive mine field, and it will feel like that at times especially if this is new to you. But it is just proof, evidence that you will be shown time after time after time, that the only answer is; to let go of ANY assumptions and just go with and work with what you see in the moment. Doing this enables you to find your solution, it allows you to be in the right place to allow your intuition to guide you, as I have said before, the problem and the answer have different energetic frequencies, you cannot find your answer while looking negatively at the problem.

When I first came to Hannah, I was very excited to explore my new home and meet my new horse friends. Hannah said I had some things to work on too, as other equines found me just as objectional as she did, so it couldn't all be her needing to change. I say we are all in her reality, so if you don't like what you see, change how you are perceiving things, human!

At first, with me, Hannah's thoughts were that if she and I did not gel together, if we did not have personalities that got on, that she would happily train me a little and then allow me to go on to someone who I would get on with. She justified these thoughts with the belief that she was not the one and only, or the best, and that I may very well be happier with another human. But she was not at all prepared for the simple fact that I immediately claimed her for my own, squealing with delight at her arrival to the yard or field, jamming my big old face up into hers, refusing to do as she asked, but refusing to get out of her face too. I had become responsible for that which I was trying to tame! She knew very quickly that even if she could not do anything with me, I, like

Mr H Bear would be with her for life.

Our first rub was to do with what Hannah had learnt from Henry Bear and other humans about love. There is no disrespect to Henry at all here, in fact, he taught Hannah the first part towards being able to unconditionally love, because he made sure she knew she could trust another. There is not one more trustworthy than Henry Bear of Bear Island. But because he would amiably go along with any of her plans, she still loved conditionally; Henry had just never given her any reason not to love him, oh! What a shock to her system bringing home a Washerpop was!

She, along with most of you didn't really understand what love is, so she went along with what she did know; the idea that all you can do is show love and kindness, (don't get me wrong, this is not a bad thing.) and then hope that that love and affection is reciprocated by the object of your attention. Most of you do that. But this is the problem here; if you are working just on that premise, then you are always going to be disappointed or feel unloved by the object of your attention when the time comes, and we all know it will always come; that time when you disagree on a subject. When the other wants to do something other than what you want them to do.

That disappointment, that unloved feeling, makes you push harder for the love you want to be returned to you, or, it makes you shut yourself off from emotions that you find painful to deal with.

And that is the opposite of what you would be doing if you hadn't become so skewwhiff in your thinking. Each negative feeling comes in you, to show you when something is out of alignment for you, out of alignment with your true nature and spirit. Each happy, harmonious feeling, be it ecstasy or peace or satisfaction or laughter, shows you are in alignment.

Quashing or squashing or ignoring your emotions leads to a build-up of negativity, frustration, guilt, anger, burying these feelings is not the answer to not being "irritated by every rub."

There is another way, and that Is to use your emotions as you were intended to use them, to guide you, to show you where you have discord between what you are thinking and doing and what your true nature wants for yourself, and most importantly; knows you can easily have.

If you can begin to know that you can use your emotions as guidance, this is where you can start to see a problem, or something unwanted appearing in your reality as an opportunity to learn from it, understand it and then you can be at peace with it and watch it disappear.

It took Hannah a long time for this one to sink in; every time she would be rubbed, wrankled, and taken out of her loving, open minded space by an action of mine. When I would go from showing my loving self to showing my 'bite the human in the head' self, or my 'I can touch you but you can't touch me' self, the frustration in my human would appear. That anxious feeling would rise in her throat, her thoughts would get racing; "God! I love this horse half to death, I know he loves me, I am being kind, I am considering how he feels, I am secure and calm when approaching him and still, still, still he is not trusting me enough, WHY, WHY, WHY! What in god's name do I have to do!!!"

I only had to bite her in the head about a half million times before she realised that what she had to do was simple, she only had to stop minding every time I showed my sharky-ness to her and then I would have no need to show it. Ta! Da! Do not be irritated by every rub.

How did she manage to "not mind" when I would blow a raspberry in the face of her studiously well thought out, considerate plans? Well partially when anyone has put up with that same thing over and over, they just get sick of minding and let it go, that's what Hannah did, but you don't need to go this far or take so long as my delectable human did, for now you have gained some knowing from Washerpop; the master of playing the devil's advocate. My pleasure, thank you, I don't mind one bit. (I am taking a bow here)

Simply know, that if something feels bad to you inside, it is showing you where you can be polished.

In Hannah's case, she had promised herself she would show infinite patience with me, and this in itself caused a problem; you cannot be perfect and even tempered all day every day, not even I can do that, and I am a very magical creature. Making unseen promises like this piles on the pressure. The universe will show you every single time, without a shadow of a doubt, if you make that kind of grand statement, the universe will bring you all and everything so that you can prove your statement to be valid; "yes, I have infinite patience as the world falls on my head". Jeez, I know one thing for sure, and that is that you humans know how to make life very hard work for yourselves! Why would you ask for that?

Striving for perfection makes you unreasonable. It sets you up against peace and harmony because you will always need for something in your life to be made perfect. I know this does not appear to make sense at first glance, but saying you will always be kind and patient, is striving against peace and harmony because you are setting an unachievable goal unless you want to go live in a white room with nothing in it.

The same happens with viewing yourself as good. For you to be good, there has to be some bad in your world, evaluating everything as good or bad leaves little room for you to see everything else that is there; the wonder, the awe and the beauty. We will always have contrast in our world, without it, we would not know how good it feels to have the long green grass to eat in the spring after a lack of it through winter. We would not appreciate the warm sun on our backs if we had not stood in the wind and rain.

Look at the warped view a lot of you have about the weather! You watch reports on what it is forecast to be; you moan if that prediction is for wet or cold, even if you have lived for a long time in a country that always has a lot of wet cold weather! You may as well complain that you woke up this morning only to find that your feet have five toes on each one, yet again!! You moan if the forecast is wrong! You seem to have forgotten that the weather is the weather! The rain and sun keeping you and us and your planet alive, and some of you have no thanks, no gratitude for that.

You have enough things already in your world to rub up against and then you go and invent some more things in your head to grind against, like judging the weather as faulty!

It has to be OK with you, for another to show you their range of emotions, not just the ones you perceive as good, without you resenting them for showing it. It is like when you are not satisfied to see all of the weather; the sun is only good enough if it never takes a day off from shining on you? Really? The rain is only acceptable if it keeps you and your planet alive without being seen felt or heard? Really? Such conditional love.

I was only showing Hannah my biting and walking away to show her she needs to work on her response to that. Once she could allow me to do something that may be out of line with what she was hoping for from me, without judging it, then I had no more need to show her that. Do you get that? Letting go of attachment to an outcome allowed what Hannah wanted from me to be present between us because she was no longer blocking the very thing she wanted.

Harmony cannot be forced, it has to be allowed. Have gratitude, ask for peace in your life, make a conscious decision next time that something rubs you, to let it go. Maybe that irate driver that cuts you up on the road; by all means, get cross that such assholes exist and have not yet driven themselves in their cars down a big hole never to be seen again. Or you can decide to say, oh well: "maybe they are very late for a job interview, perhaps they are rushing to a loved one in the hospital. Maybe they do not feel they have the luxury that I do, of not feeling so pressured in life that impatiently rushing everywhere is normal". Tell yourself: "I do not need everyone around me to drive their cars entirely correctly 100% of the time because I am in control of my own emotions and do not need to find happiness outside of myself or in other people's actions."

This is your work; to be able to be peaceful inside, to be able to come to us and others with humility if you want to smoothly glide through life and have the enjoyment you came here for.

CHAPTER 22

BALANCE

Don't throw the baby out with the bathwater

Every time we change our minds on where we stand on something. Every time we become more understanding of how we can be kinder and fairer and show more respect and consideration for the other beings in our life, we can end up swinging so far the other way that we can end up with the same kind of problems but just on the other end of the stick. There is no balance on either end of the stick; there is balance in the middle.

You do know this, because, at the moment in your human world, you have extremists and fundamentalists. And please do know, the people that react with negativity against these ones are extremists too. They are just on the other end of the stick, both proclaiming themselves to be so right, that they are justified in hating, while most of humanity are wanting the balanced place in the middle, the tolerant ground. The middle ground is where there is no fight to be fought, because no one else is doing someone an injustice, we can all get on with living and loving. Bringing up young ones, and doing what we know is truly at our essence; to thrive, to allow and assist others to do the same.

Hannah was deciding she would combat my aggression with a promise never to get angry herself, but that just made it so that more and more situations came up to test her on that.

She metaphorically threw the baby out with the bathwater, and grabbed the opposite end of that particular stick, no balance there. I followed her around the field taking out electric fence posts as she put them in. I would wait until she got nearly all the way across the field with a bucket of water for soaking our sugar beet before I took it off of her and tipped it out on the ground. She would fill up various water buckets, to offer me ones with calming aroma drops in, I would tip these out and whack her and Henry Bear on the head with them, and then chew the handles off of the buckets.

If she came to see us all clean before going out for the evening, I would take a big mouthful of my dinner and put it in her hair.

Ah… she promised never to be angry, but I did not want her to walk on egg shells, holding back unwanted emotions, to be frustrated, any more than she wanted me to be. So, I showed her I could spend the rest of my life driving her nuts, or she could let go of that idea she had about being such a virtuous angel, and admit its ok to get cross sometimes.

Now that she no longer holds in or stifles her emotions, through fear of being judged as unkind, or fear of becoming something she detests in others, she grew such a relaxed feeling of well-being in her stomach that she just sits in wonder and awe sometimes at this beautiful feeling inside of her. That ease flowing through her became apparent when she let go of all sorts of crap she had been carrying almost all of her adult life on so many different subjects.

Now, this is the kind of human I can relax with!

And the other beautiful thing my human started to notice, in finding this balance and being able to feel, and then let go of what irked her, is that; if ever that feeling, that knot of discomfort starts to re-appear, Hannah feels it straight away and knows there is something she needs to let go of. Usually, for her, something has crept in where she is starting a worry about how she is perceived by others, due to an action she has taken or something she has said.

But what used to be such a constant feeling of unease in her stomach is now so rare as to be immediately taken notice of and my sweet human can adjust almost immediately. It is very easy now, for my Hannah to know that any other being's perception of her does not define who she is and so any worry can quickly be abandoned, and the freedom from traps created for her in her own mind is the most precious thing she has found. Of all of your human strivings, this freedom from your own judgements is the best thing you could strive for.

CHAPTER 23

EVOLUTION

"The cosmos is within us. We are made of star-stuff. We are a way for the universe to know itself."

~ Carl Sagan

You humans, have a funny idea about evolution, based on what your scientists think they know. All of us are evolving very quickly right now, people and horses and all of life, this is speeding up as momentum is gained all of the time, like a snowball getting bigger and faster as it rolls down a hill.

Look how much you humans have evolved in the last few hundred years, who would have known you would be flying around the world on aeroplanes, going nuts when your Wi-Fi goes down and asking your small children to fix your technological problems because they seem to be born knowing how to do those things.

It can be assumed that evolution is just physical development, that which you can see with your eyes, but evolution is in the spirit and the mind first and foremost. You see with your eyes that your horse hasn't sprouted wings or a unicorn horn, (yes, we know you all want that!) So, you think we have not evolved much, past human interference with our breeding to produce sports horses, and different colour coats, all of those sort of things, but we have changed considerably, as have you.

In fact, none of us can stop evolving, as we create our lives and shift into what we have become.

That fish, millions of years ago, that popped his head above the surface of the water and wished to know what it would feel like to experience being on land, his thought, his desire preceded his growing legs and apparatus to breathe air and subsequently stepping out of the sea. The physical thing would not have happened without the desire. The Wright brothers thoughts and desires for powered, controlled flight came before their drawings, experiments and actual flights. Both of these are examples of evolution.

Henry Ford famously stated that he did not ask people what they wanted because they would have said: "faster horses", only he could see a car before it existed. He knew his evolution and revolution needed to be his own and not what others thought was best; this is ingenuity and innovation at its best. An individual listening to their own inner guidance.

We are all riding on the backs of, and continuing on with the evolutionary path set in motion by our forbearers; the spirit/souls of those passed, invisibly lifting and inspiring us whether we are consciously aware of that or not.

You see that there are troubles in your world and mean people are doing horrid things and then you think that progress has not been made, that things are getting worse. But that is not the case; you would not have evolved to make motor cars without horses being your transport first. You would not have developed kinder and more helpful training methods, and indeed now some of you even questioning whether it is right and fair to train us or ride us at all, if things were not getting better all of the time. If we had not evolved right there with you and guided you down that path of what we want for ourselves, it could not have happened either. We have also changed to have greater emotional intelligence and more significant needs and wants. Both human and equine evolution has been and continues to be a co-creation.

And as has been proved out in your human development over the last few hundred years, evolution is open to the snowball effect. Some of you may want to un-evolve, in that you are finding that a simpler life leads you to greater happiness, but it does not have to be either/or. You all benefit from innovation and evolution past and present, new medical technologies and other technologies that bring you closer to that self-sufficiency that will enable more and more of you to break away from convention and live the life of ease that you seek.

Some of you are frightened by the fast pace of change, trying hard to keep things the same, berating the moving away from tradition and what is known to you, but none of us can trust that what was written about or discovered one hundred years ago, or even today, will be relevant tomorrow. Hannah used to do everything she could to keep things the same, coming from a fearful view that change would be for the worse. The real reason Hannah sought and found me, is because she was terrified of Henry Bear popping his clogs, and could not bear the thought of that inevitable change occurring at some point.

There is no growth in the belief that we know how to be and are unchanged by the world around us; we are aware of everything, even if it is not on a conscious level; we sense what humankind is purposed towards. Yes, we beasts do acknowledge the darker side of how some humans feel about the animals and their earth and that they are not taking care of it. But we also sense and see so many more of you finding that your material things are not bringing you the feelings you desire, but that opening yourself up to compassion and inclusivity is. We beasts ask for more for ourselves, from your species, and you continue to evolve swiftly, the time when the scales will tip in favour of equality and peace on our planet comes ever closer now. Feel the excitement of your times.

We as a horse nation would like you to know this and take this message forwards with you; all is well. Because in this knowing, you will be able to step forwards in your world with more joy and happiness, with a knowing that every step you take, you do make a difference. The power you have to make a vast difference for the greater good of us all is very much something to celebrate and feel good about.

CHAPTER 24

SEEING BEINGS AS WHOLE

Jake Sully: I see you.

Neytiri: I see you.

Avatar. James Cameron (2009)

I changed right in front of Hannah's eyes. Physically. Twice, and only briefly to begin with. She shut these experiences out at first, not able to process what her actual eyes were showing her.

When she could look at me for long enough, without seeing crazy mixed up Washerpop; when she could look at my physiology without judging it to be unsatisfactory. When she focused purely on my wholeness of spirit, my delightful inner being that brought her such joy, the physical reality she saw with her eyes started to morph into what she wished it to be.

My legs straightened, the angry wasp's nest in my heart seemed to have dispersed.

The first time was when I was having a shiatsu healing session; to begin with I fought the feeling of the shifting of blocked energy I had carried for years, it felt alien and uncomfortable as it started to move, but then I gave in to the feeling.

What Hannah then saw in me, as the pain I had carried flowed out of my body and as the human eyes looking upon me were full of pure love and nothing else, she saw what I was to become, not just a physical relaxation of my body, but she saw a self-assurance that comes, when no point is needing to be proved, she saw a well-developed even musculature I had not up until that point been in possession of. She saw that the worry lines above my eyes that do not even disappear as I sleep, were no longer there, and she cried a few tears of joy, for she knew then who I was born to be, who I could be in any moment, without all of the negative things the humans interference had brought to my table.

The second time she saw me change, Hannah had decided to not look at the problem of my in-turned front feet and my permanently tense neck and shoulders, for another reason. She had moved Henry Bear and I to live out in a field, she had no facilities, no hard standing of any sort to be able to easily trim our feet. Doing my feet was not an easy task at this time even with good ground. Hannah had gone through a series of farriers who were not keen to return and deal with my so called 'nonsense', so she was trimming our feet herself.

It was winter time and she had been getting the job done of keeping our hooves in good shape by tending to them when the ground hardened during dry or frosty periods, otherwise there was just too much mud to be able to see what she was doing.

Then we had a spell when it just rained, and rained some more, for months on end. The bottom half of the field had turned into a lake, and Hannah knew our hooves were getting long and that she should tend to them, but she could not see how she could get it done, and in feeling completely helpless about the situation, she did what you responsible ones would call neglectful, and closed her mind off to the problem. Completely. She could not bear to think about something that caused her pain, that she felt unable to change.

And then of course, as it always does, the days and nights came when the rains stopped and the ground began to dry, and on visiting us one morning Hannah noticed as she came to the gate and I came trotting over, that the mud was no longer around my fetlocks and she could see my hooves. As I neared and slowed to a walk, she blinked and blinked again; she saw that my front legs and hooves were completely straight, hooves a little longer than she would have liked, but straight.

I am not messing with you here. She ignored these two experiences to begin with because if what had happened was true, she had experienced what you muggles would call a miracle. Hannah was not sure how she felt about that, stunned and speechless for sure, but she did want to consider if I had just sent her completely off the deep end into proper bat-shit craziness. Maybe the rest of the world was right, perhaps she was certifiable. But she did know that previously, if my hooves had gone untended for longer than optimal, that I would in fact end up more crooked.

However, in her uncertainty about what her eyes had seen, in her need, as you humans do, to look for the fault again that may no longer be there; she started to look for what she didn't want. She mentally poked at it with a stick, which is why me being able to show her my whole/best self, was fleeting, to begin with, it came and went. Until Hannah got, it, then she knew she had to look only for what she wanted and acknowledge that, and not let any other reality to have a conversation in her head; to not let those negative thoughts lead her down the unwanted road she had travelled too many times, that path that made her feel like she was walking through deep and treacherous mud.

If you see the spirit of a being, if you see their wholeness, then you enable them to become that whole being out here in physicality, to become complete; perfect, as in body, mind and soul/spirit in harmony, this is what we are all wanting to achieve with our time here. But the problem here is humans find it very hard to ignore a problem; you think it makes you dumb if people believe you haven't noticed and done something about a concern that is staring you right in the face.

So you look at it and talk about it. You think it will make you neglectful not to battle a problem. But you will never find your answer while fixating on the problem because the problem and the answer have different vibrational frequencies, focusing on the negative of a situation will not bring you a positive outcome.

Hannah had thought that I Washerpop had a self-fulfilling prophecy that was going to play out for me; she perceived that I thought the world was crazy dangerous and that I would somehow bring disaster on my head with this outlook. I did like to play with electricity and try to get out onto the road. And I ate lightbulbs and had random strange illnesses and incidents in my life. She still does not know how I broke my tail and I won't talk about it either. So she had a problem, a question that needed an answer, how can I stop this scenario from playing out?

With Hannah looking at me and focusing on the rather alarming kamikaze personality trait I seemed to be in possession of and thinking of all the different ways I could and probably would end myself through misadventure, she was not able to see the answer, she was not able to see my wholeness. Do you understand? My wholeness was and is always there, so is yours, but it cannot show itself if the eyes on it see imperfection/faultiness or chaos. If we can see the whole, the beauty and perfection that is there inside, first, and know it is there, then seeing something as whole before it takes on its physical wholeness is what enables that occurrence to happen.

It simply is just there for you if you stay present. These moments of presence were when Hannah began to see the whole of my beauty. Without judgement, without worry, without looking at the problem; my front legs straightened, my self-destructive tendencies disappeared. This is how "miracles" occur; not miracles, but the only thing that is the possible outcome when you will not accept anything else as your, or into your reality. These 'not miracles' are unlimited and available to every single one of you at any time.

What is this madness you speak of Washerpop? I hear some of you thinking; how? How can we not perceive what is there in front of our very own eyes?

After Hannah began seeing the glimpses of change in me, and then actively kept her mind off of unwanted and onto everything pleasing that she could see, and knew was to come, she saw how things could be different also with her mother, who has terminal cancer and Alzheimer's. A double whammy.

In conversation with her sister, Hannah was finding that she and her sibling were sometimes experiencing very different versions of their one and only mother. Hannah, having practised seeing me as whole, seeing my spirit and not the supposed physical or psychological defects, was also proceeding down this route with her dear sick mum. Partly because it was the least painful thing to do, to see her spirit, her gumption and sense of humour, rather than to focus on her crumbling body and erratic mind.

She very much wanted the last interactions she had with this wonderful woman who had brought her into the world, to be full of love and light-heartedness; it broke her heart to see fear, confusion and struggle in this one. Sometimes, like with my hooves, the only way you humans can stop looking at the problem is when it actually becomes too painful to look at, but it does not have to be like that if you can become aware of how your thoughts shape your reality, you do not have to wait until things in your life are too destressing to look at.

Hannah found that on visiting her mum, if she had prepared herself well, meditating on all the good things about mother and setting her intention for a great experience for them both, and if Hannah had been able to maintain her positive feelings, her mother would be lucid and physically able. She would be upbeat, and they would have a great time together.

But when Hannah spoke with her sister Alex, she learned that this one was mostly having an entirely different experience in her interactions with their mum. At this time, Alex was finding their mum to be depressed, uncertain of herself and visibly going downhill in body and mind.

Because Alex lives much closer to their mum, she has been the one to attend hospital visits where of course, the illness was the topic, and she also had the strain of being the one to always be "on hand" so to speak. Unintentionally Alex was going to her mother feeling quite burdened, helpless and down about the inevitability of a bad situation, and mother was showing Alex more and more helplessness and deterioration in spirit and physically. Hannah, on the other hand, (not always, but mostly) was visiting and thinking of finding the joy that she still could in her mother; she knew no matter how bad things got, that a joy could be found, and so she did! she looked for the sparky energetic being she knew was still inside, and she found her almost every time.

These sisters were both seeing the same person, so how could this be? each sister saw what they expected to see and so had radically different experiences.

Because Hannah had the experience behind her of what happened when she did the irresponsible (in any rational person's eyes) thing, and refused to look at, or think about the state of my legs and feet, full stop; good, bad or otherwise, for a longer period than she otherwise would have been able to if it were not for all that rain, she knew what I had been telling her for so long was true. None of you came here to be policemen of every negative thing! to notice all of the things you do not like and look for them over and over until you have nothing else but that to carry forwards in your lives.

Free yourselves of that burden, that responsibility, it is not yours to carry! Be irresponsible! Throw your hands in the air like you just don't care! If you free yourself, you will free the object of your attention also, because in your need, your feeling of responsibility, to be the 'fixer' of somebody or some situation, your object of attention has to be broken. Your thoughts and feelings on the subject have to change first, for you to see the change that you desire, for the good to start to peek it's nose into your reality.

Do you know what one of the things is that my human loves about me the most? Apart from my bare faced cheek, delectable shnozz, and nonchalant tail? She knows without a shadow of a doubt, that I never ever, even for one minute, stopped seeing her wholeness. No matter what she did. By being held in that light, in that space, day after day, she could let go and allow herself to be sucked down the rabbit hole, Into her own life, into her whole self, into everything she ever wanted. Us beasts do that, you know.

CHAPTER 25

TRUST IN NATURE

"I like it when a flower or a little tuft of grass grows through a crack in the concrete. It's so fuckin' heroic." ~ George Carlin

Human beings have become too far removed from nature, from understanding it, how we are all a part of it, all connected to the earth and how nature can give us all we need.

The animals, the plants and trees, rocks and oceans all have something to tell you and they all will give to you willingly anything you wish, if you are to ask and then listen. But you would need to trust in nature first.

You have come instead to believe that human intervention in nature is required. Management, micro management. You think that unless you mess with it, it is incomplete, not capable by its self of successfully flourishing, even though there if proof all around you that all in nature has the capacity to do that.

You put horses on little patches of short green grass, because, you say; "there is too much grass!" so ridiculous. There is not too much grass, there is a lack of vast area to roam naturally which would keep us moving and healthy, which would allow our natural metabolism to work properly. A human messed with the environment. Often grass is reseeded for one variety and fertilized and sprayed with chemicals. More messing. Could you trust in nature, if you found a big space of a variety of grasses and wild plants and terrain, could you trust that nature could do a better job of keeping your horse healthy than you, and let them out there?

Laminitis is a man-made disease, created by keeping animals in an environment far removed from what nature intended for them, and then you can make that even worse by taking us off of our small patch of grass onto a grassless smaller patch or stable, to only let us graze for shorter periods of time, meanwhile our metabolisms are getting slower, working less efficiently with all that lack of motion, so the minute you put us back on that short stressed out grass, we get sick again. A vicious circle created and perpetuated by human disconnect with nature and your need to chop everything up into small pieces and niggardly dish it out as you think best in your supreme intelligence over us.

Nature gives us wonderful coats, that perform perfectly in natural conditions, we thermo-regulate; a drop in temperature will automate a response for our coats to fluff up and trap more air, (and more body heat) warmer conditions cause our coats to flatten and release heat quicker.

But again, this marvellous example of nature working so beautifully gets interfered with by you humans making things better for us, on a small patch of land we do not move and cover the distances we would naturally, our metabolism and natural way of heating ourselves through movement not able to serve us, so you see us standing in the gateway getting cold and put coats on us. The coat offers warmth, but reduces or incapacitates our ability to thermoregulate, so you bring us indoors, or feed us more grain or sugar. Now your interference has created another circle; we come out of winter carrying more weight than nature intended and having a body over loaded with sugar and onto that fresh spring grass. Then you moan...oh! Spring, we have waited all winter for this and now laminitis, now I must worry my little head off about this.

We are designed to put on weight in the spring and summer and then use those fat reserves to keep warm in the winter months. Many problems are caused for us by the lack of natural living conditions that is considered normal and completely acceptable by most equestrians.

Your dogs, children and horses are all supposed to be much more active than is generally allowed for them, children expected to sit still at desks all day long and are pronounced faulty if they find this stillness difficult, Dogs driving your nerves to edges because they have maybe a half hour to an hour exercise out of 24 in a day and then do not easily settle into your pattern of sedentariness.

Some schools have eradicated ADHD in their children by increasing outdoor break times by one third. For years, people have been labelling their children as faulty and drugging them and, oh! Guess what, they just needed to be able to run free a little more.

Nature is a marvellous thing, you humans think you need the expensive drugs your big pharma companies make to fix your many, so very many illnesses, but there is nothing that cannot be fixed by something that grows in nature, not one thing! and many of your ailments and diseases, and ours too, would not exist if we were not getting so far removed from knowing what nature is and how to allow the flow of wellness that is our natural state, that you all have mostly disallowed yourself.

I spoke before about how when we are aligned with our world around us, when we can become aware of how everything is taken care of for us, in our alignment, we can relax into being who we are meant to be, like with the orchids growing in our field, there is no effort needed for them to thrive and for us to thrive in the same space.

Do you think maybe this is a concept you can begin to understand? You humans view nature as being competitive like people are, humans are competing for resources, for space, for better jobs, for each other's affections. You look at nature and think it is made up of the same competitiveness, animals eating each other and plants vying for space and light and water, but it is not, nothing in nature is competing against each other, each thing is being, doing its unique thing.

You view everything from the same small perspective, just like with different varieties and colours of people you deem some better than others. Just like you name some plants weeds and some flowers, there is no difference here, it is bigotry whatever thing the bigotry is aimed at.

Do you know a dandelion and root will cure many a serious ailment, but you would rather go to a job you do not like, to have money to pay the pharmaceutical industry for a chemical alternative that will poison you just as much as dampen your illness symptoms? Then you look at the dandelion and you go buy more chemicals and eradicate that plant, because it is not worthy of being on your lawn. Just so; how you name some animals as pests or vermin, how is a pidgeon vermin and a Robin not? How is a hamster a pet and a rat vermin? How do you think you can ever eradicate war and inequality in your human world when you cannot live and let live a dandelion, pidgeon, wasp or a rat?

Your view, that nature is competitive and so therefore your competitiveness as humans is perfectly natural, is a complete fallacy. Nature is creative. What do you think the difference is here? What is wrong with competitiveness? In nature, there is no need to get to the top of a pile, a flower doesn't grow the most beautiful bloom it can to be better than the other flowers! It just creates itself, it just grows and lives and enjoys the experience of being a flower.

You humans cannot possibly understand your wholeness, your oneness with everything, your part as a piece of nature, whilst you so happily separate yourself from it.

CHAPTER 26

OPENING YOURSELF UP

"Today you are You, that is truer than true. There is no one alive who is You-er than You." ~Dr. Seuss

We love you for being human; we do not need you to act like another horse, a leading herd member, for us to understand you. We understand the energy that oozes from you; we know your intention. Always make sure you come to us with the best energy that you can, that is all you need to do.

Some of you humans think being human is bad, something to be ashamed of. We believe that you should be proud; we are mainly no longer beasts of burden thanks to your brilliant brains that have invented vehicles to do your running around jobs. Your endeavour to understand our physiology and psychology gives us good, long lives, vastly improved nutrition and technology and advancement in medical care that means many of us have a chance at life in circumstances where we previously would not have.

I would not be writing this book if you lovely humans had not evolved so much.

There is only one thing you need to do, to be open to seeing our true spirit, seeing us as we truly are, as we see ourselves. Make a decision to try to let go of all the human preconceptions you have, not just the ones you may think may be unhelpful, but question all of them and start anew.

Start each day afresh by bringing yourself into the present moment, question what you believe and why you do things the way you do. Some of Hannah's preconceptions as I have talked about came from the best of intentions, she was very well-meaning, and they were born out of wanting the best for me.

But hanging onto thoughts of me being broken or faulty, needing fixing, needing a job. All of these preconceptions had the consequences of putting enormous pressure on Hannah and myself. I wasn't prepared to diminish myself and get soaked in the disappointment and frustration projected out to me.

I wasn't prepared to be viewed with eyes that told me I was broken, not whole and needing to conform to what the humans dictated is a "good" life. Think about what you really want, I said it before, but this one is worth drumming home, you may not think you are that pushy parent who finds their child's talent and then projects them at warp speed down that path regardless of all else.

But a lot of things human beings dress up as being necessary to enable their animals or children to be able to cope with the harsh reality of life, are just telling them that; "I accept mediocrity and rules are necessary to get through life, so you need to learn that is the way of things too".

Can you see how this projection takes away from the joy that is to be had in life? This joy is there for the taking, for all! Can you see how you end up nurturing a fear based culture? All fears surrounding how you or your animals or children will be perceived by others, all fears that unless you have complete control of their behaviour that they may be a danger to you or others is so false. It takes away choices for both parties. It makes your world grow smaller and smaller. If an animal understands what you are asking and loves you, they will always do their best to ensure a safe outcome for you both, that is a given, but they cannot do that if your fears are predominant and over-ride all else.

Notice how you feel; if you are not in the habit of seeing the subtleties of your own changing emotions, how are you to witness and act on those nuances shown to you by your animals or other humans? People can open their mouths and say "hey! You just hurt me with that lesser thought you just projected onto me" but mostly they won't because people are trained to suppress emotions, formed from an early age that to say this would be rude, selfish, sissy, not grown up, you may get laughed at or ignored.

Train yourself and your horse to express emotion, not just the good ones but the bad ones too. Did I tell you how delighted I was when Hannah first praised and congratulated me for rearing and spinning and squealing and bucking around her in the field, instead of projecting her feelings of fear and how this was inappropriate onto me? I was so cross before at being told I should hold it all in or go away!

How would Hannah know that I felt completely violated to have my legs and feet handled by a human if I did not feel able to express myself for fear of consequence? Horses get labelled as problem or un-trainable when it should be perfectly acceptable for them to say to you; "I don't feel comfortable with doing this thing right now." If you took your small child to learn to swim and they said that to you, would you explain to them that there are certain things in life that are non-negotiable and then push them in? No, well I hope not. But you maybe see how this is the road many horses in training are pushed down.

Every time something isn't working; something is giving you or your horse a bad feeling, stop. Stop for a second, a minute, an hour, a day, a month or a year. However long it takes for you to be able to approach in a better way, a different way from a different place in your mind.

If you start to practice mindfulness around your animals, it will not be long until you only need that second. Do not try to push through negative emotion. It will pop back up in the same place or somewhere else if it gets suppressed.

That being said, please do know that if you just ignore a problem for a year and come back to it with the same mindset in a years' time, nothing will be different. Hannah knows that; I had a year out in the field, and I was very keen to do some human stuff again after that, but Hannah had the same mindset as before, the same fears, she only started thinking differently when she saw nothing had changed because she had not left those worries behind.

Know while on this journey with your equines that you can't get it wrong because we will show you when something needs to change, and after reading my book could you not listen now? Every time we show you something that grates or grinds against you, you have another opportunity to look and see why that is and make the change within that will then reflect in your energy and actions.

Another thing to always keep in mind along the way is that your work will never be done. All of us are always evolving; there will always be a problem to be solved and a new challenge presented. The human trait of looking for the time when everything will be perfect, and you can rest leads to frustration at never being where you want to be.

Enjoy the journey; enjoy the moments, the times when we show you how joyfully we hold you in our hearts. Know that as you achieve things, what you want and what we want will change. I have already talked about this, but it is important to know that. You all watch people who do not care so much about our happiness, and you sometimes see them having an easier time of it than you. We see this too, they are not twisting and turning themselves inside out, about what is right and what is wrong, what is kind.

I and all of us would like you to know that it is supposed to be easy. Being caring does not have to carry a heavy burden that is wrapped up in rightness and wrongness. You can let go of that by just observing each and every moment and seeing what comes to bring delight.

Get over any shock or indignation you feel every time we repeat something you don't like.

For nearly three years! Can you believe that; all the things Hannah learned from her interactions with me and still three years later, she was shocked when I gave her the shark eye and bit her in the head!

She would say things to me like; "Washer, I could not be kinder to you! When will you ever seek to mind others! When will you learn that it is good to treat others how you would like to be treated!" She is hilarious.

And I am like "jeez" I'm just checking if you are over your indignation yet, and I guess the answer to that is a NO!". One day I did say sorry, it's not something I think any being should have to do too often, we should not be afraid to express how we feel, although Hannah and I can still disagree sometimes about how things are shown!

I said sorry because I was giving Hannah kisses on the lips and as she smiled, I had tried to pull her front teeth out with mine. She had kept telling me how she was going to get my teeth taken out one day to put an end to me biting everyone and everything, so what did she expect from me, knowing me so well! An eye for an eye Miss Davidson!

After I had got clonked on the nose with the plastic fly spray bottle (this is the height of violence that my person can dole out), I came and licked all up her arms and lovingly licked the side of her neck. She seemed triumphal that I had felt the need to atone on this occasion, the first time ever! but then, of course, I had to check if her indignation was still there, so I bit her in the neck! Right in that bit between the neck and shoulder, I heard her tell someone later that it was like a Vulcan Grip, whatever that is.

The stupid thing is, is that Hannah had known for a long time actually what the answer was for me not to bite her anymore. But that last bit of human instilled rightness/ safety/ indignation would not let go of her for a long time, the excuse of reacting harshly because she had a right to keep herself safe, was the resistance which made me bite her more. She knew she had to have no reaction at all to a nip from me, for me to stop. No response may sound crazy, "how will your horse know right from wrong if you do not let him know it is not acceptable to bite?"

Well, because he does already know. If you have already told him something is unacceptable and he still does it, then he does know, he just has a reason not to listen to your request. Telling some more at this point, is only likely to get you more of the same unwanted. I know it is easier said than done to let go of this control, but you can do it.

You will quite happily put up with your dog that always barks at people coming to your door, for years! Each time you will yell at the dog! Each time indignant! But it does not seem to occur to you to find out what the dog is saying and do something towards changing how he feels about people coming to his door. And you know why you don't because then you might have to change something you are doing and something you are believing. You may have to admit you are doing something not very well. So, you would rather just yell at the dog to shut up, several times a day for the rest of your life.

If you would like to see some positive change somewhere in your life, learn to recognise that nothing can change if you are not prepared to take the lead, to look at what you need to do differently to create a different outcome. You will need to be prepared to look inside of yourself for answers, not look outside and just wish others would be different so that you can be happy.

It may sound scary to think of making some changes in yourself, but ultimately, like my human has found, it is very liberating to find you can do something yourself, about unsatisfactory things in your life.

You do not have to wait for your fairy grandmother to come along with her wand, you have your own wand.

CHAPTER 27

BE FUN, HAVE FUN

If you are not having fun, you are doing something wrong. ~ Groucho Marx.

Hannah compares me to her little niece; she too can suss out adult humans very quickly and without any fuss or bother put them right straight away.

At five years old, if mum was stressing, little Hattie would say; "let it go mum". If you are boring her, she just looks straight through you and walks off, I do hope the adult humans do not make her feel this truthfulness and openness must be hidden in case people think she is rude. You grown-ups spend hours listening to all sorts of nonsense you would rather not hear, just because you do not wish to be thought of as impolite! Hannah would bore me with her training methods sometimes, and I just yawned straight in her face each time! She was so offended by me doing this at first, so as with everything else, I did it lots more until she knew without a shadow of doubt that she was boring me and had no right to indignation at my honest response.

If you expect to train me and you have no intention of making the training fun for me, then I am not going to participate. Or I will join in but I will make my own fun, there is always some fun to be had. Biting the other horses as they pass me in the arena, is fun, so is grabbing the arena lights in my teeth as I trot past and pulling them over the fence, and then pretending I am terrified because the lights attacked me. I know how to have exquisite fun keeping you goofballs on your toes, and you are the goofball until you are willing to meet your equine on a level playing field, part of which means not boring us half to death!

Convention says; 'naughty horse, untrained horse, needs telling horse'. Hannah noticed in most instances that I didn't play up, or bite, out of not wanting the interaction, or wanting to dominate, I only nibbled on her when I thought she needed to listen up and lighten up! She could feel it emanating from me if she was starting to take us, or what we were doing too seriously.

The backs of her knees would get nipped, or I would nuzzle around her neck and head, and then 'Washer Shark Eye' would make an appearance. And of course, if Hannah took this nibbling/biting as a sign that she needed to get more serious with me, I would show her, her wrongness once more. I have never feared being chastised, and at first, Hannah thought this was because I had been in this position with previous people, and just knew the score and knew not to react to that, but I always did know my right to thoroughly enjoy myself and my time on this planet in my horse suit, which is why all humans have had the same difficulties with me, no matter which stance they took, goodness me! What a shock for you humans to meet one such as me, who is determined to shine, to enjoy, to laugh and to say; "and who do you think you are? bringing such seriousness and drudgery to me and expecting me to swallow that tedious, tasteless pill?"

I will tell you this; I pushed Hannah to the point of wanting to shake me until I would stop, she did try to strangle me once, but I enjoyed that too, and it loosened a crick in my neck. Other humans would comment to Hannah, and she knew it to be true; she was far more patient than the average person, but she could see how bored I was with patience and calm and sensibleness, with no room for fun.

She could completely see how she, and others had gone down that road of trying to teach me some respect, and how that idea is flawed and with I, Prince Washerpop, a fruitless exercise. I loved seeing these shifts in Hannah's beliefs, and when I saw a tiny sprinkle of love and openness chip away at those old paradigms she had going on about achieving and telling how it should be and thinking she knew what was best for me, then my heart sang for the whole world.

My darling person knew if she admonished me for biting that my answer would be; "Oh! So, I bit you because you won't listen to my needs and your reaction to that is to ignore the meaning of my message some more! and then get bit some more; to create a never-ending cycle of unwanted behaviour which you have to ignore or justify to a certain extent otherwise you would need to think about what you are doing. And you guys believe that you are smart!" I would always just stand there: ears forward; looking straight at Hannah, never flinching, or taking any offence at any harsh words or crossness directed at me, just waiting, knowing my human could, with enough evidence from me that she could not disagree with; she could get it right.

In this world you have grown in, you have been trained to respond in certain ways. If another person or an animal does something you feel is unacceptable and you do not do anything about that, you think that you will get walked all over by others, that you must punish unwanted behaviour to eradicate it. This kind of thought takes humans off down the wrong road, the road of looking outside of themselves for others to please them instead of looking inside to see what can be done differently, to see how you could listen better. If Hannah scolded me or ignored unwanted behaviour from me, it didn't make the unwanted behaviour less happen less often. However; not pushing her crappy human idea that because she thought she was nice to me, I should happily go along with whatever she wants; now dropping that outdated idea got me listening right up and happy to play nice.

If something has stopped being fun for you; halt yourself right there. Take out of the equation what you think you should be doing and remember we all came her to enjoy the fruits. Not just to slog through the mire.

EPILOGUE

By Hannah Davidson

Go! go on; go and take some time, and just be with some of the wonderful beasts on our planet, be it a horse, dog, cat, rat, toad or a bug. Be brave and open your heart, kick the status quo in the teeth and trust that these animals may know more, than anything that anyone on two legs could ever tell you or show you. They know the secrets of the universe that our scientists are slowly trying to unravel. They will readily share these things with you if you meet them on equal footing, and get quiet and listen, and then you will be in for the ride of your life without having to get on anyone else's back to find your exhilaration and enthusiasm for life.

We are energetically connected to all life, but we are incredibly connected to those that we love and who we spend time with each day. You know that feeling when you are with a person who you connect with in this way, and you finish each other's sentences, you know what they are going to say before they have said it? We have this going on with our animals too, the communication is just unspoken on their part, and depending on our level of awareness of it, we can consistently receive that back and forth, the delightful energy exchange, I bet you all have felt it at one time.

If we are busy thinking about what we will get for dinner on the way home, while we brush our horse, we may not pick up on a subtle communication/feeling he is sending out to us.

If we have come from work or home in a rotten mood after an argument with somebody and are running through what happened in our thoughts, its highly likely your equine will not want that kind of negative energy near him at all, and this is the reason why you almost always have a crappy ride if you get on your horse in that mood. Your horse cannot easily communicate with, transmit to, or receive that jagged energy about you, it does not allow for flow and connection.

I thank you for reading this far, and hope my darling Washerpop's life views have cracked something open in you, like it did with me. I wish to convey to all, how we are truly blessed to have the animals that we do in our lives, how I have come to know that every life is to be cherished, every single one. Our beasts can teach us everything we need to know, not just about them, but about ourselves and life, how to live our lives to the fullest without fear and anxiety, but with love, joy, certainty and peacefulness.

They can show us these things because they have not become so far removed from their inner truth, as us humans have by making our world so complicated, under the misconception that coping with so many things, thoughts and feelings makes us the in clever ones. We humans are the race who are ailing and sickening more and more, as we try to juggle one more ball, and one more ball, until the inevitable happens and they all come crashing down.

Put those balls down before you get that far. Then start by only picking up the ones with joy written all over them. Give yourselves permission to find and follow you own personal bliss.

These are the lessons Washerpop has taught me, lessons that have changed my life completely and given me such a complete sense of where we all fit into this beautiful universe, that I now have a life I could only dream of before.

I have noticed, listening to a lot of different people on their spiritual journey's, that the ones who are struggling to identify and find out who they are inside and what they really want, are the ones who don't spend much time around animals or outside in nature. And being around a variety of animals is important because our domesticated animals have different things to teach us than our wild ones, they are all individuals, as are our plants and trees who also have much and more to give us! Often, a tricky problem I have been looking for an answer to, has been solved, whilst idling under the big old bows of an oak, or staring up into the soothing canopy of a willow, softening my mind, just listening to the breeze, these trees silently imbuing me with the knowledge and clarity I needed to happily proceed with what was on my mind.

One time Washerpop had lost a shoe, and I had spent a considerable amount of time looking around their field for the shoe, I gave up, and on catching Henry Bear to bring him in for the night, I said: "Oh, Bear, you will know where to find Washer's shoe, can you find it for me please?"

The next day, I had completely forgotten my light-hearted plea to Mr Bear, and on calling them to the gate that evening, Washer came, but Bear stayed planted to the spot, way across the field. At first, I wondered what was wrong with him, and then I remembered I had asked him to find the lost shoe. I walked over, and let out a squeal of delight, as there on the ground, right in front of where Bear stood, was Washer's shoe.

Time and time again, my animals, the trees, the weather, all of nature in fact, has shown me how much we under-estimate them. How, they are wanting to be in partnership with us humans, how, they know life is supposed to be easy, and if we do not separate ourselves from that, we can indeed live in an all-inclusive universe.

Our animals don't care if we wear designer shoes or drive a flashy car. Indeed, they do not care if we are stockbrokers or bus drivers, they care if we are kind. Horses tend to show us very clearly where we are out of alignment with our true self; they very much want honesty and straightforwardness from us, they know that when we are out of alignment our kindness disappears.

After I realized the extent in which we can communicate with our horses and dogs, our domesticated ones, I became very interested in trying to communicate with all different species, I was very excited to see what responses I would get from different creatures, in particularly our wild ones.

I found that a butterfly, wasp or bee would very gratefully take a step onto my hand when offered help from being stuck indoors, bashing up against a closed window. All I had to do was let them know that I am friendly and peaceful and wish to do no harm, but do wish to help and put them back outside into the fresh air. I knew I did not need to fear being stung by wasps and bees now that I could clearly communicate my intention and allow the creature itself to decide whether to trust in me and accept some assistance.

A frog, a bird and a grasshopper have all calmly accepted help from me, out of various sticky situations and have stuck around for a little while after being freed, as if to give some thanks.

But the most astonishing experience I had with a wild critter, was with a little red admiral butterfly.

I was at work one day, outdoors on a farm, another person there that day, was very cross about something and in their irritability and unconsciousness of their surroundings, this person accidentally trod on a poor little butterfly. I had seen before how when some people are in a dreadful mood, only bad things seem to happen around them. As this person stomped off complaining, I noticed the butterfly flapping in a panicky circle on the ground; one of her wings had gotten completely broken off.

I picked her up, thinking I really should just put this broken one out of her misery, but even with one so small and unlikely to survive anyway, I did not like the thought of taking a life. The second I sat her in my hand she calmed and stopped flapping, so not knowing what to do with her, I put her up on a ledge in the barn, and continued with my work.

Once I had finishing for the day I went back into the barn, I looked at the butterfly, her wing mangled so badly, and thinking she would probably be dead soon, I said goodbye. And as I did, she popped herself off of the ledge, tumbled to the ground, climbed onto my shoe, and proceeded to climb up my leg.

Ohhh…. OK! I thought, I guess I will take you home with me then, and see if there is anything I can do for you. I scooped her up, she sat quietly in my hand to the car, where I placed her on the passenger seat. And as I started on the drive home, I watched as she climbed down from the seat, across the central console/gear stick, onto my foot and back up my leg! little Wingy sat on my knee all the way home.

When we got home, I put her in my bedroom and got her a watered-down honey drink, she very much enjoyed that and I was utterly mesmerized by her wonderful snork nose (proboscis) that unfurls for drinking. I got on the internet and learned that you could indeed fix a butterfly's wing with some patience, a steady hand, the right glue and a spare dead butterflies wing. I didn't hold out much hope that little Wingy's wing could be fixed, as over 90% of one wing was gone, but I thought I could look out in old sheds and things for a spare wing, if she didn't die in the next day or two.

She perched herself on the side of a cardboard box in my bedroom, and I didn't know on that first day, that she was going to make herself into my good friend over the next six weeks.

I asked if her if she was in pain, and got the feeling back that she was not. She would get a little frustrated when the sun would first shine through the window in the mornings, she would have a try at flying then, but that was all, she would try once and then not try again. She could go anywhere she liked in the flat, or leave through any of the open windows, but she chose to sit on the box, and in the evenings when I would paint she would climb down from there and come and sit on the top of my easel!

That first night when I went to bed she climbed down from my easel and climbed up onto my bed and settled on the bottom corner of my duvet! I said to my Wingy; "you can't stay there sweet one; you will accidently get knocked or squished in the night!"

And so, I got up and put her back on the box in the corner, but she climbed down again and walked over and climbed back up onto the exact same spot on my duvet, so I left her there. Wingy would come and sleep with me in that same spot on the bottom corner every night.

I did not really know what to make of this slightly odd friendship we seemed to have instantaneously made the minute I picked her up from the ground that day, and I can't fully explain in words how her mere presence made me feel somehow better inside, it was the kind of friendship you would strike up as a kid, be it with a bug, a dog, another kid or an invisible friend; the sort of instant nonverbal bond we don't really form so much as adults, usually wanting to know quite a bit about a person before we are willing to expose our feelings with them, to risk opening up our hearts.

A couple of times during these six weeks, I had events to attend which meant I would be gone from home for a day or more. I explained to little Wingy that I would not be back until the next day. On the first occasion, I said goodbye to her and gathered up my things, I locked the front door, and walked down the two flights of stairs from my flat, and as I was walking along the road to my car, I felt a tickle on my leg and looked down, and there she was walking up my leg again!

The stealth like qualities of this one winged butterfly were astonishing, my tiny mission impossible friend, she did not want to be left out! And so, she accompanied me on these trips, again I would put her on the passenger seat and she would climb up onto my knee, happily sitting there whilst I drove for hours, basking in the sun shining through the windows, and apparently not put off in the slightest by my rather suspect singing along to the radio, or my driving skills that go to pot when challenged with roads and places I do not know well.

I looked back and thought, gosh, Wingy does make a better travel companion than most humans I know! And she did exactly the same secret attaching to me, on my way out the next time I left for a long trip.

About a month into this easy, un-spoken friendship, I was sitting one evening having a few of my favourite drinks; Jack Daniels and Coke. I was remembering a time; as a child, I'd had a hamster and had gone to my Dad one day distraught and in tears that my hamster had died. Father had said; "don't worry darling, I think I can fix him" and with that, he went to the cupboard and got a bottle of whiskey out! Very rarely did anyone drink in our house, and the Whiskey was for special occasions such as Christmas, or the odd celebratory event.

Dad poured a tiny drop of this Whiskey out of the bottle and onto his finger tip and then dripped the small drop into the hamster's mouth, and we watched and waited. Miraculously in front of my eyes my hamster did a little swallow and woke up!

I was amazed as I watched him get up and go for a mooch along the sofa, saying hello, as he always did to the family dog, with a kiss on the nose. At the time, I thought my father had performed a miracle and brought him back from the dead, but as I grew up, I realized that the hamster had probably gone into hibernation, as they naturally can do in the winter, and we had simply woken him up with a drop of Whiskey.

Coming out of my reminiscence and back into real time, I wondered if my Wingy would like a drop of Bourbon? I went to tip a small amount into her honey feeding dish, but ended up tipping rather more than I meant to, nearly a teaspoon full! She eagerly stuck her lovely curly big proboscis into the liquid and started snorking it up. I thought, oh well, if I have given her too much, it might not be a bad way to go, what with that wing too far damaged and all.

I watched as she slurped the whole lot up and then passed out, conked out on her side; she didn't even curl her nose back up into place like she usually did after drinking. I thought I had finished her off. And this is why I rarely drink alcohol these days, I mused to myself; because I do dumb stuff like this! I said goodbye to Wingy and said sorry that I had been unable to fix her wing and set her free again, and then I went to bed, three sheets to the wind myself.

I awoke in the morning and as my blurry eyes adjusted into focus, I had a little one winged butterfly sitting on my nose! Wow, I thought; Wingy, you can drink your own body volume in alcohol and far from being dead, you do not even appear to have a hangover! This one's zest for life was unstoppable!

From that very first day that she climbed up my leg and asked to come with me, she like Washerpop had made me hers. I marvelled once again at how beasts of all shapes and sizes, unlike us humans, do not wallow in self-pity and tell all others that they come across, about the woes that have befallen them, they simply adapt to their changed life circumstance, and take the pleasures in life that are still available, even if they are vastly different from the ones they had before.

Many years ago, a workmate and I had gone early one morning to the field, to check on some horses in our care, when we got there, it was obvious from quite some distance away that one of these horses had a very badly broken leg, the angle was terribly wrong, but much to our shock and surprise, he had his ears forward and was just grazing along with the herd as if nothing was wrong. He greeted us as usual, with ears forward and a friendly nuzzle and then just went back to grazing. We left him to graze, just watching him, as we called for a vet, who came and confirmed what we could see, that there was nothing that could be done for him. It almost didn't seem right to call time on him, as the horse himself did not seem to have any issue with the circumstance of having a broken leg.

If it were not for the things Washerpop has taught me about life, nature and our animals, not just horses, I would not have been able to have the wonderful connection I had with this butterfly, I would have continued to see them as beautiful, and appreciated them, yes, but I would not have known of the vast spirit and generosity that lays inside of each being, be them butterfly, wasp, tree or horse or any other consciousness in physical form. Each of us has a larger than life, bigger than our physical selves personality. Us humans are so used to making ourselves small; less than our great big expansive, true selves, that we can seldom imagine that these small beasts have everything and more to offer us, and will freely give to us, if we meet them in the right place for them to be able to do that.

I hope that, by being Washerpop's interpreter for this book, that his thoughts, feelings and ideas will help you to know what I have discovered; that we are all one, there is always friendship and beauty to be found if we allow for that by not superimposing ourselves, and our beliefs onto the other beings around us, if we can have enough humility to reconsider our long-held view that the human race is a superior one.

In this era, right now that we are all living, the contrast is stark. Those that are bigoted in their views seem to have come to the forefront again when the greater number of humans on this earth, had kind of assumed that the days of overt racism, sexism, homophobia, despotism and a whole lot of other 'ism's' and 'obia's' were in our history, and that the lessons had been learnt, (for what are known as 'first world' countries, at least) only for us to find that tolerance of all different kinds of beings appears to be at an all-time low in some minds.

Washer wanted his views known, which is why this book is written, but my input is strong also, and my message, if there is one that we can all take on deep into our souls, so as not to be forgotten, so as to make a positive difference as we are propelled into our futures, is that our tolerance and acceptance and then embracing of those who may be different to what we have been schooled to believe is in an acceptable range, cannot and does not start at the higher levels of battling fear and ignorance against these different human groups, we have to start somewhere else, we have to start at the grass roots of bigotry.

If we want the kind of world where everyone can thrive, the kind of world that is actually quite easily achievable with the level of education and technology we have today, if we do not want corporate media and shoddy politics leading people down a compassionless path for their own war mongering and profiteering motives, then we each individually need to start at the grass roots of our own ethics and question where we are truly coming from, because I can tell you, we all have work to do here.

So here we go, grass roots level;

Fertilizing a rose and spraying a dandelion with weed killer is no different from what happened in the Nazi concentration camps less than one hundred years ago, and that kind of fascism is again being fostered under today's current political climate.

How on earth are humans going to be able to accept different humans, to help and comfort refugee's instead of shunning them, to embrace the transgender, to not objectify women, when they cannot let go of the perceived threat to their step on a mythical ladder that doesn't even exist? even when it comes to a dandelion sprouting on your perfect lawn, or a wasp in your house or a squirrel in your loft? Why is a bird in your garden to be fed and nurtured through the winter months and a rat to be poisoned? Ohh... that rat will multiply and over run you, just like those darn asylum seekers?! You think this is different from the killing in those concentration camps? it is not. It is grass root acceptance that you have a right to vilify and destroy life that is at odds with your perspective.

We humans throw away between forty and sixty percent of our food in supermarkets, and then again at home and then turn and say to any other in need;

"sorry! We can't afford to keep you too! This is my ladder that I got myself on, there is no room on it for you! Sorry, but you will have to go somewhere else or, yes, just die".

Try these words, feel how they sit with you; "Corporate media and our politicians have instilled in me, a fear of you, (brown person, opposite religious person, gay person, wasp, rat, dandelion) so now I feel justified in turning off my compassion and turning my back on tolerance and inclusion, and these higher powers are happy too now, because I and most others are so switched off, that they can freely create more war, safe in the knowledge that they have whole nations of people fearful of doing anything to disagree with that"

Traps put up to kill wasps, but flowers planted and campaigns started to protect bees. We will only help those who we think can do something for us. You have allowed society to dictate to you what is a threat to you and not decide for yourself, by seeing if a compassionate way will work first before saying, sod it; "kill them all! they are plague and pestilence, these ones"

Oh, and the higher powers I speak of are not just your governments, they are your chemical sellers, they are the pharmacists, your biased main stream media, all designing your life for you in exactly the same way; creating an environment where a gaping fearful lack is portrayed, be it a lack of money, resources or health, all of which have been engineered to benefit them at a great loss to yourselves as individuals, to the detriment of our beasts and planet.

Our governments, media and big pharma are all acting in exactly the same way, they are using the same simple formula;

1. create a problem; extremists, poor health, disease, germs.

2. Fear monger through the press; bigoted, one sided, news reporting.

3. Offer the solution; advertising of product to cure, again, designed to make you fearful of one single germ or rouge cell, when in fact we all know that how we build immunity to disease is through low exposure.

In fact; this is how a vaccine works.

Can you not see the cycle?

I know you can all throw well thought out arguments at me about why we need to use pesticides on our crops, and such like, but do you know how come I am so certain there is another way?

We are fed a thought that a growing human population cannot be sustained without the use of pesticides, but have you thought about how very many more are dying from cancer caused by chemicals, and heart disease and diabetes, and the like, caused by not living in harmony with nature? So how are chemicals the answer to keeping all alive?

Aside from that, if we believe our intelligent human brains can shape something better for ourselves and our beasts and planet, then the will to do that will cause breakthroughs to happen. What stops evolution into that direction is apathy and accepting of these low standards of just surviving, instead of thriving, for ourselves.

How can I take this on board and still live in the world that surrounds me you may think? well a start would be to know that if you think you are the superior race who has a right to poison or kill other life, then you should know that you ought to be the ones with enough intelligence to solve a problem with one you think to be a pest, in a kind way, using your intelligence?

I have no desire, and we do not have to, go back to picking weevils out of our biscuits to live life without chemicals, I do not propose going backwards instead of forwards, you will not catch me living in an unheated shed without WiFi, no matter what kind of hippy you may think I am, and we do not have to, to align ourselves with nature once more.

If you understood the basic law of physics, that like attracts like, then you would know that to show kindness and compassion to these ones, will get you kindness and compassion in return.

You cannot become wholly accepting of others on a large scale when you cannot be accepting of smaller perceived slights in general, just like someone who is 100kg over weight cannot wake up the next day being their ideal weight, they need to adjust the views they hold about diet and exercise first to be able to start on the path of becoming that which they wish to be.

If we managed to eradicate the wasps and rats and flies and cockroaches, would we get down to the last few and then say; Oh...we must stuff some of these in a zoo, they are nearly all gone? What is the difference, here between Nazism and this? Would we suddenly see their importance to our eco system and give them protected status? Just because you cannot see what good a beast does (like you can see that a bee makes you tasty honey, and pollinates plants) does not mean that they do not add something, and quite frankly even if they did not, again, humans needing something or someone to prove their worth before you will consider their life to be of value, no matter how small, is human arrogance on a grand scale, just because it has been learnt and most would agree with it, just because it may be a 'societal norm' does not make it right.

To those of you who have not been comfortable reading this, perhaps, unexpected political rant at the end of a book, a book you may have thought would be a lovely fluffy old tale of a cutie pie horse and his dipsy hooman; ha, ha! I got you, you fuckers!!!

Washerpop will be proud of my tricksy-ness, he has taught me well, and I do not apologize, and he would not either, because what I have stated above is wholly relevant to us as a human race, and pertains to all that he has shown me.

Washerpop and I say: come, come with us, come with Henry Bear, and the trees, and the wind, and all other life, let us be your friends, let us bring you into your own, whatever your uniqueness may hold. Design your own wings, make your own flight.

You all have a brilliance inside of you, find it, bring it out, and unashamedly show it to the world.

What do you wanna do? Who do you wanna be?

ABOUT THE AUTHOR

Washerpop is a horse, a brown one. He does not have a unicorn horn
and wings, but he is a very magical creature none the less.
Find Washerpop on Facebook:
https://www.facebook.com/Prince-Washerpop-the-1st-
1792420567752878/
Twitter: https://twitter.com/PrinceWasherpop

Printed in Great Britain
by Amazon